Build a Brand Like Trader Joe's

Bikewriter.com

ISBN 978-0-9791673-3-1

Acknowledgements

Mary Pinizzotto was the first reader, a sounding board, and helped to shape my thoughts and this book. It can't be easy to be married to a writer. When I'm working, what I'm doing looks exactly the same as if I were just aimlessly surfing the internet, staring out into space, or doodling.

Thanks to Nihan Yesil, proofreader.

Two good friends, Harry 'Brammofan' Mallin and Jim Carns both, at different times, listened patiently while I worked out some of the ideas in this book and spent hours reviewing the manuscript. They've been great supporters of my writing whether the subject is motorcycles or not.

Mark Eimer, my advertising partner at *re:* designed and photographed the cover. For more information about *re:* go to www.revolutionaryoldidea.com.

●

Disclaimer

This book was not unauthorized by Trader Joe's. No Trader Joe's employees, present or past, contributed to it or were even aware that it was being written.

Warning

Canadians are famously polite people. Strangely though, most of us have real potty mouths. There are about a dozen instances of the words 'fuck' or 'shit' in this book. (OK, fourteen if you count those two, but it's still less than 0.05% of all the words in here. My 85 year-old mom swears more than that.) I write in my own voice, and I won't insult my readers by replacing 'uck' with a string of asterisks and pretending it's somehow different. If you can't handle the occasional expletive, go back to the Kindle Store and return this book right now; Amazon will refund your money.

Foreword

These are the first few pages of this book, but they were written last. A year ago, the first Trader Joe's employees transferred in to Kansas City to open the first Trader Joe's store in this market. I worked there for most of that first year.

☞ **I did not apply for a job at Trader Joe's in order to write this book.** I applied because I thought, *"Here's a business with a great reputation and loads of fans—there are 5,000 people on the 'Bring Trader Joe's to the Kansas City Metro' Facebook page, for God's sake—it's growing fast; it might be cool to enter on the ground floor and see where it takes me."*

Until I came face to face with them, I didn't understand how devoted Trader Joe's customers are to the brand. 'Cult' is not too strong a word. If Trader

Joe's was not so publicity averse, it would certainly have a place on Millward Brown's 'BrandZ' list of the 100 most valuable global brands.

From the first moment we opened the store, Kansas City went bananas (19¢ ea./regular, 29¢ ea./organic) for Trader Joe's. Given my advertising background, I couldn't help but marvel at the way its brand equity had been created without advertising or, even, a recognizable brand strategy.

"Trader Joe's must," I thought, *"be getting everything else exactly right."*

Then, as the Grand Opening crush subsided and we got down to business as usual, I saw a company that, like so many of my old advertising agency clients, just muddled along. Studying Trader Joe's revealed far more 'worst practices' than best ones.

☞ **That was when I knew it was worth writing** *Build a Brand Like Trader Joe's.*

Imagine a typical business with a mix of strengths and weaknesses, but that also has a solid brand strategy and a creative ad agency — you'd expect such a company to have brand equity and devoted customers, at least as long as they kept pumping money into the brand. You wouldn't bother writing a book about it; it happens all the time. It's the advertising industry's *raison d'être*. Totally expected.

What about great brands built *without* advertising? Obviously, those are rarer, but almost every successful small business is built on referrals, without a brand strategy. I can't think of too many *eight billion-dollar* businesses built that way, but conceptually I can imagine an amazing company, run by geniuses, doing everything *but* advertising perfectly. Such a company would make for tedious reading, and the book would be useless, too, because ☞ **"Do everything perfectly," is not practical advice.**

•

☞ **I wrote this book because there's a valuable lesson to be learned from a company that hasn't even got an ad agency—*and* functions with merely average core competence—*but* has still managed to build one of America's strongest brands.**

The fact that the Trader Joe's I experienced first hand was mediocre in so many ways was, paradoxically, why I knew other companies could benefit from emulating it. All I had to do was divine The Secret to Trader Joe's cultural brand equity. Once I had that, I could present a list of best practices short enough to have a practical application in the real world.

That's what I've spent the last year doing. (Well, that and talking to thousands of customers, bagging a million dollar's worth of groceries, and stacking several tons of bananas.)

●●

You know how when you're in the supermarket and you can't find an item on your shopping list and you look and look and finally you stop a clerk and ask him and he reaches out without taking a single step and puts his hand on the can of beans or whatever it is you were looking for because it was right there in front of you but you couldn't see it?

I had one of those moments when I realized that The Secret has been right in front of me for my whole advertising career, hiding in plain sight. It's so obvious, although in a lifetime in the ad business I've never heard anyone mention it.

☞ **I could just blurt out The Secret right here in this Foreword. That would save you several hours of reading. But I'm afraid you would think,** *"That's too easy; that can't possibly be it."*

● ● ●

So instead, I've structured this book in a way that mimics my own journey. ☞ **In the first part of the book,** I'll provide you with enough background on Trader Joe's, and on me, to share my perspective. ☞ **In the second part of it,** I'll delve into the culture of Trader Joe's by examining Trader Joe's own published values, its Mission Statement, and letters from CEO Dan Bane to Crew Members. I'll help you understand what the company says, and what it does —those things are often quite different. I'll help you sort out which of those defining traits most shape the brand. ☞ **In the third part,** I'll sort through what we've learned, postulate a cultural brand theory to explain Trader Joe's success, test it against things we know are true, and ☞ **lay out a three-step plan you can use** to build a great brand of your own. (There's actually four steps, if you count, "Don't completely fuck up everything else," but that goes without saying. I mean, it's The Secret; it's not magic.) ☞**At the end of the book,** assuming you'll want to apply what I learned, I'll outline a few pitfalls in Trader Joe's approach to cultural branding, and provide evidence that Trader Joe's itself has, at best, an imperfect understanding of its own success.

●●●●

Oh, one more thing: For the record, none of Trader Joe's confidential information is revealed in this book. (How could it be? I was an hourly-wage employee hired off the street without so much as a background check; I wasn't privy to any corporate secrets.)

That said, for a company that conducts its business out in the open, Trader Joe's is obsessively secretive. So I quit before this book was published, in order to save my Store Captain the embarrassment of firing me.

The crazy thing is, for all that my time as a Crew Member involved getting up in the middle of the night to go and hump boxes, standing at the cash register processing a never-ending line of customers, or picking through the cheese display looking for mold at twelve bucks an hour... I already miss it.

It was an intense year. Enjoy the read.

Mark Gardiner
Kansas City, 2012

The beginning: Friday, July 15, 2011. Grand Opening

☞ *Opening a new store in a new market* ☞ *Drawing a huge crowd without Grand Opening ads or specials* ☞ *A brand built without ad agency help*

My alarm went off at 3:45 a.m. My breakfast was pre-made; my coffee waited in a thermos on the kitchen counter. I got up and out to the motorcycle as quietly as possible to let my wife sleep.

I did not come across any other traffic on my ride through Kansas City, but there were already a few cars in the parking lot of the Ward Parkway Shopping Center. I parked the bike in the far corner of the lot, as I'd been instructed, and walked up to the store.

Twenty or thirty people waited by the doors. They were wrapped in blankets, and slouched in a ragged line of lawn chairs.

"When did you get here?" I asked the first in line.

"About 3:30," she said, laughing.

The automatic doors were turned off but unlocked; I pried them apart and entered. A few other Crew Members moved around as I walked back to the staff room where I dropped off my jacket and helmet. I punched the time clock at the 'pit,' over by the cash registers.

Outside, dawn began to color the sky. A few more people clustered by the door, looking in. By five o'clock, the full opening crew, about 40 people, were in the store. The aisles were still cluttered with cartons of produce that had just arrived. Someone wheeled a pallet-jack loaded with banana boxes across the floor. Dairy and meat products were stacked in front of refrigerated displays, and Crew

Members worked to get them onto the shelves of the 'cold wall' before they spoiled.

Huge rolling racks of bread had to be put, loaf by loaf, onto shelves in the bakery area, and thousands of apples had to be stacked into neat pyramids. By seven, the sun was streaming through the big plate glass windows, and we could see a hundred people out there, and more arriving.

"One hour!" shouted a manager.

Crew Members started to run from task to task. The store's P.A. pounded out The Pointer Sisters' *'I'm So Excited.'*

"Thirty minutes! Make sure you're working clean!" Managers started gathering empty cartons and clearing the aisles; a couple of Crew Members ran big dust mops up and down the aisles.

"Fifteen minutes!" Now everyone was running, all the time. *'Highway to the Danger Zone'* blared on the P.A.

"Huddle! Huddle!"

Someone turned the music down, and the staff and managers gathered in the produce department by the front doors. Hundreds of people were massed outside, as if waiting to rush for front-row seats at a rock concert.

Mike, our Store Captain said, "A store only has one Grand Opening, and you guys will always remember this one. The main thing now is just to have fun with it."

Someone quickly ran down the roster of which eight Crew Members would operate the cash registers, and someone else gave us armfuls of leis to hand out to the first customers through the doors.

"And..." it was eight o'clock on the dot, "we're open!"

A Crew Member flipped a switch and the doors slid open. That was the last time we were really in control. As fast as we could, Crew Members tossed leis over the heads of customers.

"Aloha! Welcome to Trader Joe's."

Customers shopping with baskets ran in between and ahead of the ones pushing carts. In the tide of people, I caught a brief glimpse of my wife, then lost sight of her. There were mall security guards at the entrance and police in the parking lot, but they weren't really needed; the crowd was well-behaved.

We should have known that the Grand Opening would be a scene; the 'Bring Trader Joe's to the Kansas City Metro' Facebook page had gathered 5,000 friends. When we ran out of our own carts, customers pushed through with oversized Petsmart and Target carts, scrounged from the far ends of the mall.

By the time it was my turn to run a cash register, customers were basically getting into a cash register line as soon as they entered the store; they inched their way up and down the aisles and arrived at the registers long after their frozen purchases had thawed.

In spite of that, most of them were in remarkably good spirits. Customers showed off bags they'd bought at other Trader Joc's stores. Many of them told me that they were members of the Facebook group or that, in the past, they'd traveled as far as St. Louis to shop with us. Another common theme was, customers had fallen in love with Trader Joe's when they lived on the coast, then had longed for it after moving to Kansas City.

Suburban moms came in and bought three or four reusable bags; a few customers *only* bought bags. (Trader Joe's bags would be the hip way to carry your yoga mats in Kansas City for the next few months.) Bells clanged as cashiers needed help, which happened a lot; nothing in our brief training had even attempted to simulate this crush of customers.

"Will the eggs always be that price?" For the nth time, I explained that Trader Joe's doesn't do sales or specials. Everything was the same price, every day. After two hours on the cash register, I was reeling.

I took a few minutes to just walk the floor. Two shell-shocked guys in suits stood in the produce department talking quietly; they had little 'Cosentinos' lapel pins that identified them as managers of a nearby grocery store. Their competitive landscape had just changed forever.

Crew Members like me aren't supposed to work overtime, so I clocked out at 1 p.m. when my shift nominally ended, but I felt guilty about abandoning the ship. I stayed another couple of hours helping to bag groceries in a vainglorious attempt to reduce the time customers spent waiting in cash lines. After a couple of extra hours running on nervous energy I realized that there was no way the Grand Opening crush would subside, no matter how long I volunteered to stay. The afternoon shift would have to sink or swim without me. I needed to rest if I was to survive tomorrow's 5 a.m. start.

☞ Day Two

The late night clubs and bars were still disgorging Friday's customers as I rode into work. There was no line of people in lawn chairs waiting for me, but if anything, the crew had more work to do to prepare the store for its second day in business. By the time we opened the doors at eight, there were even more customers waiting.

That weekend, all of Kansas City wanted a piece of us. A huge display of 1,000 cases of 'Two-buck Chuck' was bought down to the bare floor. People weren't dissuaded by the crowds and long lines either; several people came through my cash register and told me that they'd been at the *other* store's opening the previous day. (Trader Joe's opened two stores in the Kansas City market simultaneously. The other store was in Leawood, a suburb a few miles away.)

My first week's schedule called for two opening shifts on that Friday and Saturday, and then a closing shift on Sunday. So, on Sunday, I didn't start until 3 p.m. The store was packed again right until we locked the doors at 9 p.m. It fell to me to do the 'final cart run.' It was a perfect summer evening. I gathered up shopping carts that had been abandoned in the far reaches of the parking lot.

As I pushed a string of carts back to the store, a Rolls Royce rolled into the finally-empty parking lot. The huge sedan slowed and stopped, and the driver's window silently lowered. Inside, there were two middle-aged guys in the front seat; their well-dressed wives sat together in the back.

"Pardon me..." the driver said, with a dramatic pause. His friend could not quite suppress a laugh.

As an ex-advertising agency Creative Director, I knew exactly what had made his friend snort; they were reenacting the beginning of a famous television ad for Grey Poupon mustard. (The year was 1988, the agency was JWT; check it out on YouTube, it's an advertising classic.)

He went on to ask me how late the store was open, and when I told him that it was closed, they drove silently away.

I should have said, "It's a shame you're too late. Our Dijon mustard's particularly good," before the window rolled up. But I was too distracted by the profound realization that it was Trader Joe's *brand* that was bringing in customers, and that the customers themselves were brand-savvy.

It's not like I was the first guy to notice. In 2009, Landor listed Trader Joe's as one of America's Top-10 'Breakaway Brands.' (They devised the list after analyzing data from Young & Rubicam Brands'

Brand Asset Valuator.) Laurence Knight, the president of brand consultancy Fletcher Knight identified Trader Joe's as a 'brand with soul' two years before that. Dan Hill, whose company Sensory Logic has tried to make a science of understanding consumers' emotional relationship to brands, has also been citing Trader Joe's as an example of a brand that's built a great *esprit de corps* among both shoppers and employees.

Those guys in the Rolls didn't know that I knew why they were laughing. To them, I was just a twelve-buck-an-hour guy pushing shopping carts in the parking lot. But I had spent a good part of my working life in ad agencies persuading clients to invest in their brands, and promising that if they did so, their investments would yield a worthwhile return.

I should have been gratified to see my advertising beliefs supported by the evidence of Trader Joe's Grand Opening weekend in Kansas City. There was just one catch: Trader Joe's built its incredibly loyal brand following *without* brand advertising. The company doesn't even have an ad agency, nor have they built their brand according to the gospel of social media. In this Web 2.0 world, TraderJoes.com is rudimentary; the company doesn't even have an official Twitter feed or Facebook page.

So, how the hell *did* they do it? That night, when I got home, I grabbed a notebook and started jotting down my impressions. This book is the result.

A brief history of Trader Joe's

☞ *The original 'Joe' turns a convenience store into an experience* ☞ *Secrecy-obsessed German owner* ☞ *Only 3 CEOs* ☞ *Category-leading rates of sale and profit*

The original 'Joe' was a guy named Joe Coulombe. He was not a humble grocer; he was an ambitious kid with a Stanford MBA. After getting out of school, he went to work for the Rexall drug store chain which put him in charge of a new retail concept they were trying out—the convenience store. (I know it's hard to believe that there was a time *before* convenience stores, but it's true.)

Rexall's market test was a chain it called Pronto Market, a half-dozen small stores in the Los Angeles area. They sold everything from cigarettes to booze and ammunition (a great combination in L.A., eh?)

In 1958, Rexall decided that the experiment wasn't worth pursuing, and instructed Joe to shut the stores down. Instead, he bought them out. Coulombe grew Pronto Markets to 17 stores before the Dallas-based Southland Corporation expanded into Southern California. He knew that he could never compete with the marketing muscle and economies of scale of 7-11.

There are different versions of the Trader Joe's creation myth in circulation, but the gist of them is that some time in the mid-'60s, Joe took an island vacation and came back to California convinced that a generation of young Americans were traveling more, and returning home with broadened tastes in food and wine. Or, perhaps he'd been a big fan of the 1958 film South Pacific. Or, he was enamored with the obscure autobiography of Alfred 'Trader' Horn, who was a white ivory trader and adventurer in nineteenth century Africa.

I don't know which, if any, of those tales are true, but what's unmistakable is that the counterculture movement was in full swing, and Joe conceived of a laid-back store, decorated with an island theme, where the staff wore Hawaiian shirts.

The first Trader Joe's store opened in Pasadena in 1967. It was about twice the size of his Pronto Market stores, and offered a better-than-average selection of affordable wines, and specialty foods like fresh sourdough bread and whole-bean coffees that were not readily available in supermarkets. Although the first Trader Joe's was conspicuously different from current stores in some ways (it sold phonograph records and hosiery, for example), Joe's original vibe still prevails. For the next 20 years, Joe carefully honed his concept while opening about one new store a year, all of which were in Southern California.

☞ **One epochal event in the store's history happened entirely behind the scenes in 1979. That**

was when Joe sold the business to a German grocery magnate named Theo Albrecht. (Theo persuaded Joe to remain in place as Trader Joe's CEO; customers were none the wiser to the change in ownership.)

•

Theo Albrecht and his brother, Karl, were second-generation grocers who started the Aldi grocery store chain in Germany after WWII. In 1960, the two brothers disagreed about whether their stores should sell cigarettes, and they split their 300-store chain into two businesses with Theo taking the northern half of their territory and Karl taking 'Aldi Sud.' Both chains maintained a friendly relationship, often consolidating buying.

Both 'Aldis'—Nord and Sud—grew rapidly, with a rigid formula for success that hinged on minimizing fresh produce (and hence spoilage), stocking a far smaller number of SKUs (stock-keeping units, i.e., products) than rival stores, keeping stores small for minimal overhead, and driving hard bargains with suppliers by paying cash. By the early '70s, the Albrecht brothers were two of the richest men in Germany.

In 1971, Theo was kidnapped and held captive for 17 days. He was released when his family paid a ransom of 7 million German marks (about $12 million to you and me). Until Theo's kidnapping, Karl had always been the secretive one. Afterward, both Albrecht brothers lived in nearly complete isolation.

So, when it comes to companies, there's privately held and then there's *privately held*. When Theo died in 2010, Forbes estimated his fortune at over $30 billion. And yet, German newspapers had to scramble to find an image to illustrate his obituary. The most recent photo was a single image of Theo and Karl together which had been snapped over twenty years earlier. The next-newest photo they had of Theo had been taken the day before his kidnapping. (Before his death, Theo had transferred his Aldi Nord and Trader Joe's holdings to a family trust.)

••

Anyway, when Theo Albrecht acquired Trader Joe's, it was a small grocery chain operating in a restricted market. As noted, Theo kept Joe Coulombe on as CEO, and was a 'hands-off' owner. I've heard that 'the Germans' only came to the Trader Joe's headquarters once a year. The one thing Theo pushed Joe on was, he wanted Joe to expand the chain much faster. In 1988, Joe wearied of arguing with the Germans about growing the company, and retired.

As his replacement, Joe tapped another Stanford MBA, John Shields, who had already had a successful career with the Macy's and Mervyn's department store chains. (I guess Shields only wanted to work for businesses with an apostrophe in the name.)

Shields was the CEO of Trader Joe's from '88 to 2001. During that period, the chain grew from 27 stores all in Southern California to 175 stores in about a dozen states, presumably satisfying the Germans' desires for growth.

☞ **After Shields, the company got only its third (and current) CEO, an accountant named Dan Bane.** Bane was hired by Trader Joe's in 1998, moving directly into senior management as the President of the western region, and became CEO in '01. He's credited with bringing Charles Shaw wines (aka 'Two-Buck Chuck') to the chain; those wines became the stores' single biggest-selling product. Bane, too, has almost certainly met the Germans' desire for growth. With him at the helm, Trader Joe's has doubled its store count.

The Albrecht ethos permeated the Trader Joe's culture, too. Like Theo, the company became almost fanatically secretive. When *Fortune*—hardly a magazine with a reputation for hack-jobs—wanted to profile Trader Joe's, Dan Bane refused numerous requests for an interview. The company's internal web site gives an almost comically paranoid set of instructions for "what to do if the press shows up at your store." The head office in Monrovia, California, is completely devoid of any signage indicating what business operates there.

So, where does that leave Trader Joe's as of this writing?

Considering that my store was the 355th one to open, but was assigned a store number of 720 by the head office, it's clear that management feels there's plenty of room for expansion. Trader Joe's is only just cracking the Texas market, for example; there are, as yet, no stores in Florida, or in some cities (Denver leaps to mind) that would give Trader Joe's the same fervent welcome it got in Kansas City.

New stores are larger than the original concept. My store in Kansas City is about 14,000 square feet; much smaller than the average supermarket, but still about 50% larger than the average Trader Joe's store. Some long-established small stores (mostly in California) are being closed as newer, larger replacements open nearby.

In most ways, the retail concept has stayed true to its roots, which include many of Aldi's tenets. (The similarity between Aldi and Trader Joe's likely explains some of the appeal that Joe Coulombe's original concept had for Theo Albrecht.) As at Aldi, the stores are physically small and the number of SKUs is restricted. A Trader Joe's store typically offers about 4,000 products for sale at any given time, which is only about one-tenth of the selection available at a full-sized supermarket. Again, like Aldi, the vast majority of stuff sold in Trader Joe's is sold under proprietary labels.

The company is not vertically integrated. Rather, it just arranges for outside suppliers to do parallel product runs in Trader Joe's packaging. Both Aldi and Trader Joe's buyers can strike great bargains with suppliers that are chronically frustrated with the hijinks pulled by virtually all rival grocery chains where suppliers are treated as another profit center. Trader Joe's and Aldi pay on delivery.

No money is wasted on brand advertising; in fact, the company hardly does any advertising at all. There's no such thing as a sale at Trader Joe's.

The company never comments on financial matters, but I can evaluate published estimates based on my knowledge of the sales racked up in my store. (We're often told our store's daily total in the late-night 'huddle.')

The most frequently cited figure for Trader Joe's revenues is $8 billion. Although my store is one of the largest Trader Joe's, and clearly, we do above-average volumes, I'd say that's conservative. *Fortune* estimated that Trader Joe's was moving an average of around $1,700 in merchandise per square foot of floor space annually. Based on direct observation, I think that $1,700 figure, impressive as it is, grossly *understates* the sell-through in my store.

Whole Foods—a publicly traded company and therefore more of an open book—is an obvious reference point. It is, admittedly, a different business selling a larger variety of products at premium prices in larger stores. That said, judging from the number of people who carry their Trader Joe's groceries home in Whole Foods' reusable shopping bags, the two chains appeal to many of the same customers.

Whole Foods' sales per square foot are about half of Trader Joe's, but with much larger stores, its revenues are in the same ballpark as ours. (WFM recently reported sales of around $10 billion.) Its net profitability of about 2.7% makes it the leader among reporting grocery chains, but my instincts tell me that Trader Joe's is, if anything, even more profitable. My guess is that if you imagine a cash cow that the Albrechts milk to the tune of about *a million dollars a day*, you won't be far wrong. Even half that amount, however, would make Theo's decision to buy out Joe Coulombe one of the most prescient investments ever made.

So, this book is not just the story of a business that built a fanatical corps of brand evangelists without spending a cent on brand advertising; it's the story of a fantastically profitable business operating in a sector known for razor-thin margins.

You're thinking, *Now they've got some Best Practices for me to study.* In fact, I'll spend much of this book describing a business that does as much wrong as the average business—which is to say, almost everything.

Don't let that disappoint you. If anything, you should be heartened by the fact that, like you, Trader Joe's really embraces mostly Worst Practices. You see, I'm not going to present you with a whole laundry list of Best Practices that are inevitably going to prove impossible to implement.

Instead, I'm going to describe a handful of things that Trader Joe's does very, very well. And you'll learn that if those things are done well, customers will overlook any number of Worst Practices. Want to build the kind of brand loyalty Trader Joe's has, without wasting another cent on advertising? You're reading the right book.

●●●

[Author's note: You might have this reservation: *I admit Trader Joe's has built a great brand, but it's just a grocery store. Is it relevant if I'm not a grocer, or even a retailer?*

Trader Joe's is a pure, crystalline brand experience. On one particularly crowded day, I watched a woman drag her husband through the store. As they inched along, I heard the man muttering over and over again, "It's just food; it's just food!"

Everyone has to buy food; it's usually a commodity. Do you really care whether your bananas are Dole or Chiquita? Trader Joe's operates in a category that has long been driven by price and convenience, but its customers are willing to drive long distances to get to a Trader Joe's store, bypassing many rival grocers along the way. If Trader Joe's can build a great brand in such a commoditized category, it should be even easier for you.

A grocery store is not just a good place to test branding and marketing theory. It's a great place, because virtually every family shops for food at least once a week. Successes, or failures, are immediately measurable.

Maybe you're in some business that seems to be a world away from groceries, like high-tech manufacturing. Apple's next iteration of the iPad could kill your new tablet computer before it's even born. Do you think you have a strategic challenge timing your release? Try selling fresh fish, and then tell me *your* timing's critical.]

How did a six-figure ad agency Creative Director wind up pushing shopping carts for twelve bucks an hour, anyway?

☞ *Getting an education in branding at a successful Canadian retail chain* ☞ *A career as an ad agency Creative Director* ☞ *Throwing it all away* ☞ *Shopping at Trader Joe's* ☞ *One of the first 50 hired to open the Kansas City store*

I graduated from the University of Calgary in 1980, after taking a long and winding route to a Bachelor's degree in General Studies with a minor in English. Nowadays, General Studies is a hip major. Back then, I'd have done as well telling prospective employers that I'd spent the previous seven years in jail.

That wasn't a problem for me, though, because I wasn't looking for a job; I had my heart set on being a freelance journalist. I worked at that for several years, building up my collection of 'clips'. For a year or so, I published my own 'zine (before that was cool). I worked for a couple of small magazines and aspired to see my prose appear one day in *The New Yorker*, or *GQ*. (I built up quite a collection of rejection letters, too.)

In the early '80s, I paid my rent and bought food and gas with money I made selling articles to magazines, which was more than any other writer I knew could claim. But I wasn't paying anything on my student loans, which meant that I was actually falling further and further into debt. Suffice to say, my parents weren't exactly bragging about me to their friends whose sons were lawyers, engineers, or doctors.

One day, a guy who ran a small Canadian ad agency read an article that I'd written in a local magazine. He looked me up, called, and said, "I think you should come and write ad copy for me."

I knew something of the ad business because my dad had been a sales-and-marketing guy at Union Carbide. If you're of a certain age, you remember The Man From Glad. That was a character that JWT (the ad agency that made that Grey Poupon mustard ad) created to launch Union Carbide's Glad brand of plastic bags and cling wrap. My dad always liked hanging out with the ad guys; the actual Man From Glad—the actor—once had dinner at our house.

Anyway, I told that local ad guy on the other end of the phone that I was a *serious writer*; a future George Plimpton who would not stoop to prostituting myself in the ad business.

Then, he said, "I'll start you at $30,000 per year."

"All my life," I responded, "I've been waiting for this call."

The guy (his name was Steve Bottoms) ran Cooper-Hayes Advertising, a small agency that was owned by its biggest client, a Canadian clothing chain called Mark's Work Wearhouse. The first thing Bottoms did was to hand me a copy of *Ogilvy on Advertising,* which served as my formal education in the ad business.

The informal part of my ad education came from having been raised in the milieu, and then serving an apprenticeship under the Mark who lent his name to the Mark's Work Wearhouse retail chain—a foul-mouthed, cigar-chomping caricature of a Jewish 'rag merchant' named Mark Blumes.

Blumes was, literally, a larger-than-life character, becoming famous (or, more accurately perhaps, infamous) in the Canadian retail sector. Although he was the son of a medical doctor, he was a merchant by nature. He'd built a chain of men's clothing stores that, by the time I arrived on the scene, numbered 200 stores.

I worked for Mark's Work Wearhouse for about five years, first as a Copywriter and then as a Creative

Director at Cooper-Hayes Advertising, and eventually in the capacity of Vice-president of Marketing, reporting directly to Blumes. As the chain's buyers began stocking a better grade of merchandise, I engineered the transition of the Mark's Work Wearhouse brand from that of a discount outlet for blue-collar work clothes to a mid-priced, high-value supplier of work and casual clothing.

The highlight of my early advertising career came in 1988, in the days leading up to the Winter Olympics, which were held in my hometown of Calgary. I created an ad for Levi's jeans that ran in Russian with politically incorrect English subtitles. The next morning, it was the lead story on Good Morning America.

Mark's Work Wearhouse was a good place to learn the advertising and brand-building business. Blumes was passionate about his stores, and while retail brands aren't perceived as glamorous clients in the ad business, they're exceptionally responsive to branding and advertising success or failure. Mark's Work Wearhouse sold a lot of private-label stuff, like Trader Joe's, but equivalent products were to be found in many—indeed most—competitors' stores.

Blumes knew that great customer service would differentiate his brand from the lackadaisical attitudes that prevailed in the Canadian retail industry overall. Mark's Work Wearhouse also had advanced inventory control and sales reporting systems for the time. So if we ran an ad, and sales didn't tick up the next day, my phone rang that morning with complaints from buyers, regional managers, and Mark himself. On the other hand, if I ran an ad and sales went through the roof, my phone also... well, come to think of it, when my ads worked, the phone was silent. Still, I learned what worked or didn't right away.

Later on, I owned my own creative shop in Calgary where I worked on mostly sporting goods and home-building clients; I was a Creative Director for several agencies handling breweries, dairies, and General

Motors' ad work in western Canada; I was the director of marketing for a high-tech firm and managed a 20-person creative department at an agency 'back East' (as they say in Canada) handling mostly telecom and banking work. For a while, I worked at a hip shop in Kansas City called Muller & Company; its claim to fame was that the industry magazine ADWEEK once named it one of the most creative small agencies in the U.S.

After the better part of 20 years creating advertising, I pretty much dropped out of the ad business. I'd spent that time making great money and blowing much of it on an addiction: motorcycle racing. That is, literally, another story. (If you want to know about it, you can read one of my other books, *Riding Man*.) When I stopped racing, I found myself writing for motorcycle magazines all around the world — which, while it didn't pay nearly as well as creating ads for a living, was maybe the only thing even more fun than writing ads.

I kept at motorcycle writing until a perfect storm of global economic recession and the rise of web-based media essentially eliminated professional freelance journalists. Suddenly, at fifty-something, I was an unemployed ex-journalist and ex-ex-advertising copywriter.

●

I met my wife in California. When we lived there, we often shopped at the local Trader Joe's store. I noticed that there were clerks in there who were nearly my age. Moreover, the employees often seemed kinda' cool and generally happy in their jobs. As a confirmed foodie, I was skeptical of Trader Joe's produce, but overall, although I wasn't in the cult, I was favorably disposed towards the chain.

We moved from California to Kansas City, trading wildfires for tornadoes and affordable housing, in 2009. A year or so later, we heard rumors that Trader Joe's was going to open a couple of stores in our market. When the rumors proved true, I applied for a job on a whim (and because I'd heard that even employees who worked as little as 20 hours a week qualified for health insurance).

The company cut off applicants after it had collected the first thousand applications for positions at my store. They hired fifty from that thousand to buttress a couple of dozen employees they'd transferred in from other locations. I was one of the first fifty.

When I first reported for duty at the store, I was genuinely open to the prospect of spending the rest of my working life in the grocery business. It was only after I came to realize the depth of enthusiasm that Trader Joe's customers had for the brand—and that the brand had been built without advertising, i.e. in complete contradistinction to the methods I'd studied and practiced for years—that I knew I had to write about it.

Of course, given Trader Joe's fanatical secrecy, once this book was released, my work there would be finished.

Welcome to the crew

☞ *Extroverts wanted* ☞ *Ten days of indoctrination*
☞ *Values, not process*

We, 'first 50', all reported for duty on July 4. (Yes, on the holiday; perhaps it was Trader Joe's way of letting us know that the store would completely control our schedules.)

Long tables had been set up, and folding chairs put out, so that we could all sit together and fill out employment paperwork. As you would do, I looked around and took the measure of the other new Crew Members. I was almost the oldest one; that's not ageism so much as recognition of the fact that it's an intensely physical job and 99% of American 50 year-olds simply can't do it. The skew was 20-something.

☞ **Once the basic admin stuff had been taken care of, we introduced ourselves. In a random group of fifty people, most individuals would dread standing up and addressing a group of strangers, but this crew was different. Hands shot up—they were, like, "Pick me! Pick me!"**

By turns, they described college educations (humanities, the arts, teaching; several were actors). Many had a little joke or anecdote to share. We'd all been told we'd been hired for our personalities; extroverts were predominant. People quickly made eye contact, and were soon chatting comfortably with each other.

We had ten days of indoctrination before the Grand Opening. It was carried out by the experienced Crew Members and 'Hawaiian Shirts' who had transferred in from existing stores in other markets.

The hierarchy in a Trader Joe's store is simple: There are only two real 'managers' in the store: the Captain and his First Mate. (The First Mate position seems, subsequently, to have been eliminated.) The rest of the store staff are divided between Crew Members, aka 'part-timers'—people like me who wear T-shirts on the job—and 'full-timers' who wear Hawaiian shirts. Many, or most of the part-timers actually work full-time hours; the distinction is mainly that the people in Hawaiian shirts have manager keys for the cash registers and are compensated differently with better benefits.

Crew Members earn their Hawaiian shirts by paying their dues—usually for several years—working in T-shirts. The change of attire is a big deal in the company culture. New full-timers are called 'novitiates.' Feel free to draw your own conclusions about the way the company drops its extended nautical/tropical metaphor and adopts religious terminology to describe that transition into management. There's an element of accidental honesty in the choice of words.

I use the word indoctrination to describe those first ten days, because the actual training was minimal.

Admittedly, most of the day-to-day work on the floor of a grocery store is menial. But I was still struck by the ratio of time spent discussing values, compared to time spent discussing process.

Most companies spend 90% of training time on procedure. At Trader Joe's, very little effort was expended to ensure that we knew how the cash registers worked, or that there was a specific order, top-to-bottom, in which different boxes of meat were to be stacked in the huge refrigerator. (Pork goes on the bottom, then chicken, with beef on top; it's based on recommended cooking temperatures.)

☞ **What we *did* do, for hours, was listen to the Hawaiian Shirts talk about Trader Joe's company values** and the ways Trader Joe's was different from other stores. Most of these talks were conducted with zeal and sincerity (although, there were one or two long-term employees transferred in who were obviously cynical.) Experienced employees put on little two-person plays in which one acted out the role of a customer—asking a question, or coming through the cash register—and the other acted out the role we were expected to play as employees.

So, what are the company's published 'values'?

☞ Integrity

☞ We are a product driven Company

☞ We create WOW customer experience every day

☞ No Bureaucracy

☞ We are a national chain of neighborhood grocery stores

☞ KAIZEN!

☞ The store is our Brand

Surfing the load

☞*Day-to-day life in the store* ☞ *Manual labor*
☞ *Surviving and thriving on chaos*

The first thing a Crew Member does after punching
in is to check the daily log, which in my store is
posted on a clipboard near the time-clock. You find
your name on the log and read across to see what
you're supposed to be doing hour-by-hour through
your shift. One of Trader Joe's tricks to building
esprit de corps has been to create a work force of
generalists. Although there are some specialized
positions, such as being a sign artist, virtually every
employee rotates through every department.
Everyone takes their turn on garbage duty, and even
cleans the bathrooms.

That's not to say that Crew Members don't specialize at all; some take responsibility for writing orders in certain categories so they're more familiar with what's new or what may have been discontinued in that aisle. And the managers who pencil in tasks on the daily log tend to assign certain Crew Members to produce, and others to wine, etc. But, both in principle and in practice, there is nothing in a Trader Joe's store that is not your job and therefore, nothing that is not your responsibility. If you're walking past the phone and it's ringing, you pick it up. If a customer has a question, you might take them to find someone more qualified to answer it, but your answer is never, "That's not my department."

The day-to-day life of a Trader Joe's Crew Member is taken up by three or four primary activities. Most eight-hour shifts either begin or end with a few hours in which the store is closed but fully staffed. That's when the heavy lifting is done. Trucks arrive daily and drop off 'the load.' Whole pallets stacked with hundreds of cases of wine, or boxes and boxes of grocery items, are wheeled out onto the floor and broken down.

☞ **On a busy night, 50,000 items will be removed from corrugated cardboard boxes and placed, one by one by hand, on shelves to be ready for tomorrow's shoppers. In grocery-speak, this is called 'throwing the load.'**

Since most of the crew at my store were, like me, new to the job, in the early days, the managers scheduled a lot of us to stock. As we got faster, they cut the staffing back, so that in those hours when the store was closed, the pace ranged from merely exhausting to utterly frenzied.

When the store is open, of course, anywhere from two to 12 of us would be running cash registers or bagging groceries. Given the emphasis the company places on customer interaction (something that takes a degree of freshness) and the terrible ergonomics of Trader Joe's cashier workstations, no one is allowed to work the till for more than two hours at a time.

At any given time, there is typically one staffer whose only job is greeting customers, answering their questions, and generally chatting them up. In keeping with the company's nautical theme, and considering that this job is largely about steering customers towards products, Trader Joe's calls this position 'helmsman.' Crew Members are assigned the role of helmsman for one hour per shift at the most.

That means that most of the time, most of the staff are doing something else. They're throwing the load: removing items from corrugated cardboard boxes and putting them on the shelf, one by one by hand. Throwing the load while the store is open is a lot like doing it while the store is closed, except that since the aisles are crowded with shoppers, there's no room to wheel an entire pallet out onto the floor. So, Crew Members break the pallets down in the back room, and wheel stacks of four or five boxes out at a time.

Part of the magic of Trader Joe's business model is that sell-through rates are far, far higher than most grocery stores. 90% of the inventory turns every two weeks; many popular products—not just perishable produce—almost sell out every day.

This approach ensures that the store's money isn't tied up in inventory that's not selling. But, order writing is often assigned to fairly junior employees who make mistakes. Hiccups in the supply chain can leave any item out of stock in the warehouse, and even items in stock in the warehouse and on the day's order don't always arrive in time. Inevitably, even without major problems, quite a few items are out of stock at any given time. Two semi-trucks per day left the Chicago warehouse for my store, which even in good weather and traffic conditions was an eight-hour drive away. A flat tire or winter snowstorm threw the whole system off.

This could result in a store with a lot of bare shelves, which would be bad for business. The reason it doesn't look bare is that Crew Members are told to fill empty spots with products they do have. If you made a time-lapse film of a section of Trader Joe's shelving, you'd see a constant ebb and flow of products on display. That means that stocking shelves, which could seem like a mind-numbingly tedious job (and it is one) is also a task that involves making a constant series of adjustments. Is the store almost out of prime Angus steaks, but there's too much hamburger in the big cooler out back? Beef up the burger display, obviously. But what hamburger to put out? If there's more of that expensive organic ground beef, it's more likely to appeal to the sort of customer who might otherwise have bought a steak.

This process of adjusting and optimizing the products on display never ends; although there's not a right and wrong way to solve this equation, there are better and worse solutions, and hiring staff who are capable of grasping such a vague assignment and keeping them motivated to actually think about it is essential to a store's profitability. I called this, 'surfing the load.'

Learning to surf in five lessons...

I started shopping at Trader Joe's about ten years ago when I lived in Encinitas, California. My house was about 400 yards from a well-known surf break, Cardiff reef, and I surfed almost every day.

The Encinitas Trader Joe's store was three or four miles away, just across Interstate 5, and although I was aware that it was part of a chain, I assumed that the surfboard-and-tiki-torch theme was a nod to the local surf culture (which, to be honest, is really the only culture there is in San Diego).

At the time, if a Trader Joe's employee had told me, "We're a national chain of neighborhood stores," I'd have believed it, but I would have been misinterpreting the evidence. It was not until I moved to Kansas City and got a job working at

Trader Joe's in the Midwest that I realized the whole 'South Pacific' surfing decor was applied nationwide.

Still, surfing gave me a perspective on Trader Joe's success because there are several parallels between the experiences I had out on my surfboard and the experience I had on the floor at my store. One of the first things all surfers learn is that the ocean really doesn't care about you, and that it is too big to fight. You have to make the best of the waves that come your way. You can devise strategies and learn techniques, but no two waves are exactly alike. So you have to adapt over and over again to make the best of things.

In the grocery business—especially in a quick-turn environment like the one at Trader Joe's – the "load" is like the ocean, imperfect and chaotic by definition, and fundamentally beyond your control. And yet, Trader Joe's has proven to be a consistently excellent surfer. What are some of the lessons you can draw from their success?

☞ Surfing Lesson #1: Trying to be cool, isn't

Ever since the Beach Boys and Jan & Dean, surf culture has shaped America's perception of 'cool.' Surfer style is rooted in the ability to make something that is actually very difficult look effortless. Surfers are all about the next wave, so their style is an unstudied afterthought.

Surfers implicitly understand that if you're trying too hard, you can't possibly be cool. You have to be yourself, be relaxed, and be natural. Trader Joe's has maintained a consistent brand that's unprepossessing — look at the funky handwritten signs produced in each store by resident artists, for example.

☞ Even though the staff is working incredibly hard, they always make time for customers, cultivating a laid-back customer experience.

☞ Surfing Lesson #2: By the time everyone can see a big wave, it's too late to catch it

When the wave is clearly defined by a curling lip of white foam, you're too late–in fact, it's risky even to attempt catching a big wave at this point. A good longboarder, especially, is up and surfing before the wave breaks. Then he turns his board and goes "down the line," riding the smooth shoulder of the wave for as long as possible.

Don't try to drop in on whatever today's big wave happens to be. Trader Joe's claim is, "We don't follow trends, we set them." The company has been consistently good at introducing its customers to new products and at negotiating favorable prices with suppliers before a new product becomes the next food fad.

☞ **Surfing Lesson #3: If you ride your wave all the way into shore, be prepared for a long paddle back out.**

Novices are thrilled just to stand up on the board. If they get up, they usually ride the wave all the way into shore. That leaves them with a long, exhausting paddle back to the lineup. ☞ **Experts know the benefit of ending their ride early so they can catch the next wave sooner.** When they feel a wave start to fade, they turn out of it. They spend more time surfing and less time paddling.

Trader Joe's, with its limited SKU selection, is ruthless about cutting products when sales slow (or when prices rise). One of the most common conversations I have with customers is my letting-them-down-gently chat, when I tell them their favorite product has been discontinued.

☞ Surfing Lesson #4: Commit

When it's time to try to catch a wave, a half-effort is worse than useless. You won't get up on it, but you will interfere with others who are more committed and make enemies in the lineup. Commit to your wave and paddle as hard as you can; if you're first up, other surfers will yield to you.

There are many businesses that claim the customer is #1, but if you really look at their actions, almost all of those companies obviously place their customers' convenience behind their own, and even that of their suppliers. The customer is, in fact, usually #0 — which explains the current endemic of shit customer service.

Trader Joe's is different. When it tells new Crew Members that, no matter how busy they are with other tasks, they should drop what they're doing to satisfy almost any customer request, the company really means it. The cliché is that Crew Members on the floor working the load should have their heads on swivels, making eye contact with customers and inviting questions.

Most questions come down to, "Can you help me find..." and it's Trader Joe's policy—no matter how busy Crew Members are with stocking tasks – that they should never just tell a customer where the product can be found, but rather, they should drop what they're doing and lead the customer right to the product they're looking for.

An immediate benefit of this approach is that it minimizes 'phantom stock-outs.' That's grocery store jargon for products that are in the store, but which customers can't find. The much longer-term benefit is that customers bond with the brand by bonding with individual employees.

It would be more efficient for Trader Joe's to do all of its restocking overnight, when stockers can move around freely without being interrupted by customers. But by 'inefficiently' stocking during business hours—and we stock even on peak weekend afternoons—the company creates the maximum number of opportunities for customers to have those one-on-one brand-building experiences.

What counts here is not the policy, but commitment to the policy. At any given time, there's one manager who's designated as the 'quarterback.' That person is usually in the back room breaking down pallets of products into stacks of boxes about five feet tall which are wheeled out into the store by Crew Members. Although it was rare for quarterbacks to come right out and tell Crew Members to work faster, there was constant pressure to do so. Crew Members are all aware that working the load quickly figures into your semiannual review. Managers are, themselves, reviewed on their quarterbacking skills, which means their ability to whip Crew Members into a stocking frenzy determines *their* raises and bonuses.

And yet, for all that pressure to work the load—for all that Crew Members are strongly discouraged from idle chat with other Crew Members—any employee is encouraged to drop what he's doing and go on a long, leisurely chat-and-walk with any customer. ☞ **On the busiest days, any employee is more than welcome to spend ten minutes digging through back-stock to find a one-dollar item for some little old lady whose total bill is only going to be $15. "I'm with a customer," trumps any other assignment.**

If you just claim, as almost all businesses do, that "The Customer is #1" and then provide typically shitty customer service, that claim will only insult your customers and piss them off all the more. If you claim "The Customer is #1" but punish your staff for actually treating them like #1, you'll frustrate them, too.

Remember the seven values described in the preceding chapter? In the next chapter you'll learn that Trader Joe's is less than 100% committed to some of them. But it's totally committed to the idea that customer satisfaction is built up through a whole bunch of personal interactions, and that no Crew Member's duties should ever deter them from providing one of those interactions.

☞ **Surfing Lesson #5: A bad day's surfing is better than a good day's work**

Because of the fundamentally chaotic nature of the business, there's no such thing as a 'good' day when it comes to surfing the load. The order process is imperfect; it's difficult to predict customer traffic, which is influenced by everything from the weather to college basketball schedules; the warehouse will run out of key products or simply fail to ship them; the truck will be late or break down and not arrive at all, or drop off an enormous load on an afternoon when the store's already choked with customers. If it isn't one thing, it's the next.

Every Trader Joe's Crew Member confronts this brutal realization some time in the first few months on the floor: The cycle never ends.

Frustration. Exhaustion. Panic. Whatever the crew is feeling, even if it's a particularly tough day, it cannot be transmitted to the customer. Just before our Grand Opening, we were gathered together to hear a little pep talk from some regional vice-president. One of the things he told us was, "If you're ever not having fun here, please quit." It was not so much what was said that made an impression on me; it was the way it was said. After all, many companies tell new hires,

"Working here is fun!" even though very few hourly-wage jobs actually *are* fun. It's a tribute to Trader Joe's that one conversation customers usually *don't* have at the cash register is the one I've heard so often at other stores:

Cashier: *"How are you today?"*

Customer: *"Fine, and yourself?"*

Cashier: *"I'll be great in an hour; that's when I get to go home."*

☞ **The lesson you need to take away from this is that everyone at your company who is in a position to interact with the customer needs to be able to find something in the day-to-day reality of their job that's satisfying and even fun.**

This is not about instructing your employees to smile and ask customers how they are. (Trader Joe's employees are expressly told that if they're not feeling great, they're welcome to answer the question, "How are you?" honestly. To apply this lesson, you need to create a culture in which your employees genuinely care about customers.

Coming up, I'll write about the ways Trader Joe's has built an *esprit de corps* amongst Crew Members, most of whom (most of the time) will work extra hard so that when they leave at the end of their shift, the workload is tolerable for the shift that follows. If you adapt these notions to your own company and put them into practice, you'll find that ☞ **if your employees genuinely care about your customers and each other, within a short time your customers will genuinely care about your employees—and by extension your company, too.**

When that happens, it reinforces your employees' attitudes. It's a virtuous cycle, and when you get it going, you'll be building your brand the Trader Joe's way.

Zen and Art of Cultural Brand Building:
An inquiry into values

☞ *Like most companies, an imperfect grasp of its own secrets* ☞ *An analysis of values* ☞ *The Mission* ☞ *Things we don't do, that make us different* ☞ *Things we do do* ☞ *Dooby dooby do (just kidding)*

Most people, in their working lives, really only get an insider's perspective on a handful of businesses.One of the interesting things, however, about working in the ad business was I got to see 'behind the curtain' at hundreds of businesses.

Over the course of working with all those different clients, I had many opportunities to ask, "Who are your customers, and what do they like about your business?" Every business thinks it can answer that question. But when I did my own research, I usually found that my clients had at best an imperfect impression of who their customers were and an even hazier picture of what customers *thought*.

Most businesses get a still worse grade when it comes to knowing *why* customers think what they think. Ironically, businesses that are doing well are often the ones least motivated to really seek an understanding of their customers.

What I'm going to explore, in this part of this book, is how Trader Joe's has built up its incredibly valuable cultural brand and fanatically loyal following. Since a culture is best defined by its values, I'm going to structure this extended chapter around discussions of Trader Joe's own, self-proclaimed values. I'll give you an insider's perspective on just how Trader Joe's lives up to each value in turn. Sometimes, you'll learn that Trader Joe's 'values' are just words on a page; sometimes, you'll learn that even if the company lives up to a value in its actions, doing so doesn't really contribute to the brand. In the process, it will often seem that

I'm dissing the company. My purpose in doing that isn't to bite the store that feeds me; rather, it's to give you hope. If a great brand like Trader Joe's sucks at as many aspects of *its* operations as your company sucks at your operations, maybe you don't need a long list of best practices; maybe all you need to do is figure out which essential practices Trader Joe's is getting right, and do those things. That's what this book is all about.

Now, I'll work back through those 'values' and differentiating factors, and grade Trader Joe's on each one, both in absolute terms and as a function of how much (or little) each value contributes to the Trader Joe's brand.

☞ Value #1 — Integrity

> *At Trader Joe's we demand that all Crew Members behave with unyielding Integrity. The definition of Integrity is simple...it means that you treat others as you would like to be treated. Our Company is very unusual*

*because of this important and key Value. We
are committed to treating all customers,
vendors or suppliers and each other with
Integrity.
Our focus on Integrity as the first Value is on
purpose…*
—Trader Joe's Crew Member Handbook

Gardiner's Third Law of Copywriting states: No
claim is meaningful if everyone else is also making
it.

It may come as a shock to you, but during my twenty
+ years in the ad business, I helped to sell some real
turds. I wrote hundreds of ads for General Motors
dealer groups at the height of the SUV phenomenon.
Read Keith Bradsher's *'High and Mighty'* to learn
just how terrible those vehicles were for consumers,
the environment and, ultimately, the American auto
industry. It would have been incredibly refreshing if
GM had ever come to me and suggested an ad to the
effect of, *"Hey, we'll never let Integrity get in the
way of short-term profit; we'll say or do anything it*

takes to convince you to drive a great bargain...for us."

As a claim, Integrity is both universal and meaningless. But, if you're going to trumpet 'integrity,' you open yourself up to examination for it. Trader Joe's was behind the curve when it came to signing the Fair Food Agreement that helps to ensure that farm workers are treated at least slightly better than slaves. And it only moved to ensure that its fish was sustainably harvested after Greenpeace mocked it with a website that dubbed the store 'Traitor Joe's'.

The company also has a reputation for pressuring small independent producers to sell products to Trader Joe's and only Trader Joe's. This puts suppliers in a precarious position, because the company is not above discontinuing a product over a few pennies of wholesale cost. The impression that I have is that suppliers put up with Trader Joe's ball-busting because the company pays promptly and doesn't shake them down for a bunch of bogus 'marketing fees' and slotting allowances.

☞ **Upstream, Trader Joe's is certainly not worse than the average grocery chain, but it's hardly the poster child for Integrity.**

Downstream—inside the store—customers *are* treated with integrity. We don't ask to see a driver's license when customers pay with checks; we don't examine large denomination bills as forgeries. We don't have a disingenuous 'members' program that requires you to show your card to pay the posted prices.

●

When I first started working at Trader Joe's, and realized that at peak times there are always long lines at the cash register, I worried about the impact of making people wait, and had trouble reconciling the long lines of customers with the company's exhortation to chat up every customer as they came through my line.

Then I remembered shopping at the public markets when I lived in Paris. Two or three times a week I strolled through the Seventh *Arrondissment* where I lived, to colorful outdoor markets where I did most of my grocery shopping. There, I visited with my cheese monger, my fish monger, my butcher, and specialized sellers of fruits and vegetables. There was a guy who sold nothing but tomatoes; another, who sold only lettuce, still had mud on his hands from picking it that morning.

Since each purchase was a separate transaction, I didn't just line up to pay once, I lined up to pay over and over again. The best stalls always had six or eight people waiting ahead of me. The frustrating thing about standing in those lines was that the people who were doing the transactions never seemed to be in a hurry. They'd have conversations with whatever shopper they were dealing with; asking if she'd liked the *jambon* they'd bought last time, or explaining that, sadly, the last of the chanterelle harvest had passed. Recipe advice was traded. The weather, and its influence on the Tour de France came up... It made you crazy as you waited your turn. But the thing was, everything was forgiven when you got your turn at the front of the line and for a few minutes you, too, were the center of that seller's universe.

●●

When I moved from Paris to Southern California and started shopping at Trader Joe's, I had to make a difficult adjustment vis-à-vis the produce in grocery stores. Fruit and veg is not a strong suit for Trader Joe's; especially not items like tomatoes or strawberries that are picked long before they're ripe, and are prone to bruising and rot afterwards. I vividly remember buying some strawberries that sprouted a thick coat of furry white mold within a day or two. I carefully picked out and washed off the edible ones, and although I didn't expect to get satisfaction, resolved to take the rest back to the store.

I walked into my local Trader Joe's and showed the half-eaten box of berries to a cashier, who directed me to the nearest Hawaiian Shirt. I expected to be grilled: When had I purchased them; did I have a receipt?

Instead, the manager immediately opened a cash register and refunded the full purchase price. ☞ **That was an example of Gardiner's Fourth Law of Marketing: Nobody loves you as much as someone who just hated you.**

Trader Joe's accepts returns or exchanges with no questions asked. You might think that by selling me moldy strawberries that I didn't like, and then returning the purchase price, Trader Joe's was at best getting back to zero from a negative position. But in fact, the benefit that accrued to the brand far exceeded the return of the strawberry purchase price.

The reason for this is, when I saw the mold on the strawberries, I did not take it personally. I knew that if someone else had picked up that box of fruit, it would have sprouted mold for them, too. On the other hand, when that guy in the Hawaiian shirt cheerfully returned my purchase price and apologized for the mold, that was personal.

☞ **Any personal encounter trumps any anonymous encounter. If you empower your staff to do whatever it takes to make things right, every time you disappoint a customer as a company, you create an opportunity to befriend him as a person.**

☞ **Overall grade for Integrity—C**
☞ **Contribution to brand**
     (Essential=5 Irrelevant=0)**—2.5**

☞ Value #2 - We are a product driven Company

> *At Trader Joe's we have elected to differentiate our business from other food retailers based on our products, the customer experience and the overall value that we provide... Foremost of these differentiating factors, however, is our product. Our Buying/ Merchandising groups search the World over for great products that are screened for acceptance through the rigorous parameters of our unique "Buying Philosophy"...*
> —Trader Joe's Crew Member Handbook

Retail is not rocket science (unless you're talking about the gift shop at NASA, in which case it is). There are only a handful of ways that a retail store can differentiate itself from its rivals: The curation & selection of products on offer, location, and pricing of course...that's almost a complete list.

One of the interesting things about Trader Joe's is that the store only offers about 4,000 SKUs—which is to say about 10% of the number of products, sizes, and packaging options on offer at a Whole Foods store.

On the face of it, that could put Trader Joe's at a disadvantage. Or does it? In *'The Paradox of Choice'* psychologist Barry Schwartz argues convincingly that consumers are frustrated by having too many choices, and anxious about making the wrong purchase.

That limited selection could place intense pressure on the buyers at Trader Joe's head office, however. The store's claim is that—while it only has one kind of white flour, or one kind of ketchup, instead of a dozen choices or more on offer at large grocery stores—customers can count on it being one great product.

Many customers believe the claim that, when Trader Joe's stocks only one SKU of some item, it must be a great one at a great price. The truth is that while most of the items in the store are sold under Trader Joe's labels—making direct comparisons difficult—it's not a vertically integrated company, so all those products are sourced from independent suppliers and some of them sell substantially identical products under other brands at other stores. (Suppliers are sworn to secrecy, but over the years quite a few identities have been leaked. Many of Trader Joe's yogurts, for example, are made by Springfield Creamery.)

Most Trader Joe's prices are sharp; better than any regular supermarket on comparable products, on a par with Costco and beaten only by Aldi. (In the U.S., Aldi stores are owned by Aldi Sud, the half of Aldi owned by Theo Albrecht's brother Karl, so there's no direct ownership connection.) But Trader Joe's *says* it doesn't place a heavy emphasis on the price side of the value equation. It claims, for example, that its buyers don't even consider price until after they've decided whether to carry a product. In its view, product appeal is primarily the result of quality and, often, uniqueness. Trader Joe's makes a big deal of being, "...Traders on the Culinary Seas!" and seeking out new products that it can introduce to its customers.

At the risk of snobbery, ☞ **Trader Joe's is not remotely close to competing with rivals like Zabar's, Dean & DeLuca, or even Whole Foods when it comes to a selection of top quality products or exotic, adventurous foods that are new to most American shoppers.** We started to carry coconut oil only after it had been requested by many customers, so it was hardly a discovery—although once it was on the shelf, I'm sure many regulars bought it to try it for the first time.

On the face of it, you might argue that people go to the store to shop, and that the only way Trader Joe's makes money is by selling products, so the products must be good enough, and interesting enough, to bring shoppers back again and again. By that measure, it doesn't matter that most of the products aren't the best or most exotic; they're good enough for the customers the store attracts.

My instinctive rebuttal—again at the risk of coming across as a snob—is that if 'good enough' is good enough for you, I don't really want to help you build your brand anyway.

My rational response is more relevant—the claim that Trader Joe's success is product-driven, isn't supported by the evidence. Sure it's at least arguably true that my store presented quite a few items that were exotic in the context of a Kansas City suburb, but the two highest volume Trader Joe's stores are both in Manhattan—the most diverse food environment in the U.S.

The New Yorker staff writer Patricia Marx, who writes the magazine's occasional *'On and Off the Avenue'* shopping series, recently visited the Union Square Trader Joe's and found a long line of people waiting to squeeze in and shop. *"The loyalty inspired by certain supermarkets is downright devout,"* she remarked. *"Take the Hare Krishna cult of Trader Joe's..."*

Marx was unimpressed with Trader Joe's produce. *"[E]xcept for the frozen mango chunks...nothing very hotsy-totsy is going on in terms of produce,"* she noted. ☞ **One of her friends described the store as, 'the home of the lonely food.'** What she meant by that was that most customers seemed to buy single-serving prepared meals that they took home, microwaved, and ate alone while watching TV or checking their Match.com messages.

☞ ***"See the dude wearing the Hawaiian shirt, surfer shorts, and a big grin...or Crew Member,"* Marx wrote, *"he is so eager to chitchat that he gives 'friendly' a bad name."*** Is being friendly bad? Only in New York... But Marx gets close to the store's real appeal by realizing that shopping at Trader Joe's is a social experience.

The management guru Clayton Christensen, who wrote *'The Innovator's Dilemma,'* has an interesting perspective on 'products.' In his view, when you go to a hardware store to buy a 1/4" drill bit, it's not because you want a drill bit, it's because you want a 1/4" *hole*. Christensen suggests that the way to think of products is: they're something you hire to do a job.

☞ **From that perspective, clearly most Trader Joe's customers are hiring products to provide them with a convenient, at-home meal service.** It's a rare customer who comes through the cash register line with a cart full of ingredients. Most of the store's profit comes from prepared foods—including foods as simple as precooked frozen rice, or pre-made garlic toast. Customers are, unwittingly, loading up on salt and calories with most prepared meal choices.

☞ **Overall grade for Products—C**
☞ **Contribution to brand**
        (Essential=5 Irrelevant=0)—**2**

☞ Value #3 - At Trader Joe's we create WOW customer experience every day

> *We are committed to make every customer shopping experience rewarding, eventful and fun.*

—Trader Joe's Crew Member Handbook

All of us newly hired Crew Members were told, more than once, that we'd been hired for our personalities. The company wants a staff of outgoing people who (while we were cautioned not to *pester* customers) say, "Hi" and initiate conversations with customers that go beyond, "Did you find what you were looking for?"

The Crew at store #720 was well-chosen by that criterion. There are a few "motormouths" with self-confidence issues (as in: too much of it) but most of the staff are conspicuously friendly and quick with a little compliment; well-educated types capable of carrying on a conversation when it seems invited. (The crap state of the economy in the years after

2008 has helped Trader Joe's hire an impressive staff for starting wages of about $12/hour.)

☞ **One of the keys to understanding Trader Joe's success is learning to see the brand as the result of two kinds of customer experience: external and internal.** Most companies expend most of their effort on the external experience, which is made up of what the customer sees and hears (and, since it's a grocery store, smells and tastes, too). Those things are 'real' and quantifiable.

The internal experience is what the customer *feels*, as they experience your brand. Trader Joe's knows that the internal experience *"...set[s] us apart from other grocery retailers and set[s] the stage for the customer's participation in the "external experience" of shopping at Trader Joe's."*

There's a huge idea embedded in that innocuous quote. The intangible way customers feel about your brand colors the way they evaluate all those tangible brand experiences. Those tangible, external experiences—the so-called 'real' experiences—are scored on a sliding scale. ☞ **What matters is the emotional basis on which customers evaluate the real stuff.**

In the Crew Members manual, Trader Joe's tells us that customers ask themselves questions such as, *"Do they really care that I am shopping here today?"* or *"Do they trust me?"* ☞ **The manual leaves out the single most important questions of all:** *"Do they really like me, and do I like them?"*

Some relatively enlightened companies have tried to systematize a customer service process that will lead to their customers' emotional, as well as rational, sense of having made a satisfying purchase. But no matter how well you attempt to program that customer response, nothing replaces authenticity.

I often take my half-hour break at the Starbucks upstairs in the mall. On different coffee breaks, I've had the opportunity to both witness a 'strategic,' programmed bit of emotional brand-building, and to experience the lasting effect of an authentic customer connection.

An example of the first kind happened the time I was waiting my turn to order, when the barista said something rather strange to the customer ahead of me. I don't remember the exchange word-for-word, but it was something to the effect of, "We're just going to give you a moment of unexpected delight; your drink is free."

The language she used was obviously scripted. The customer blinked a couple of times, took it in, and said, "Thanks," picked up the drink and walked away. I'm sure they liked getting their drink for free, but any emotional contact was fleeting.

As I placed my order and waited for my drink, I often traded a few minutes' chat about life in the retail trenches. It got to the point where, if my break coincided with that shop's early closing on Sunday evening, the guys who were cleaning up and getting the shop ready for the next morning's opening shift would look around to make sure no one was watching and unlock the door so that I could take my coffee break in there. That was a real gesture of friendship.

Trader Joe's could just write a policy for employees working the cash registers that would say something like, "If a customer mentions that it's their birthday, don't charge them for flowers." That would be good, although many customers will already get flowers, from someone else, on their birthday. What would be much better is to have employees that were genuinely empathetic, and who walked over to the flower display and picked out a bouquet, and gave it to a customer who was obviously having a crappy day, and didn't expect it to suddenly be brightened.

☞ **A real 'wow' experience is authentic. It comes from the heart, not the manual. It's an emotional connection between two people.**

If you're a numbers guy, or an MBA who's been taught that branding is a science not an art, that's a scary thought. But it's not that hard to deliver. You need to hire a certain kind of employee — someone with empathy and judgment. Those are largely innate, not learned traits, but people who have those traits aren't too hard to find. Then, you take a deep breath and empower that person to do *what it takes* to make that customer's day.

☞ **Overall grade for 'WOW customer experience' — A**

☞ **Contribution to brand** (Essential=5 Irrelevant=0) **— 5**

☞ **Value #4 - No Bureaucracy**

At Trader Joe's we simply have no room for bureaucracy...everyone is evaluated on their contribution to the Company's mission, not to group or departmental matters.
— Trader Joe's Crew Member Handbook

OK, "No bureaucracy" might be an exaggeration. I had to sign a piece of paper that acknowledged I'd taken possession of the Crew Member Handbook, for example—not because the Company wanted it back when I left (no one asked me for it when I quit), but rather so I could be held accountable for familiarity with its contents. I doubt if the original Joe instituted that policy.

It's true, however, that there's not *much* bureaucracy at Trader Joe's. The head office only has a staff of a few dozen people. I often saw my Store Captain pitch in to help with the most menial tasks.

Although this value has only an indirect impact on the customer's brand experience, it supports that experience to the extent that, when a customer that approaches any Crew Member with any question or complaint, he is a maximum of two degrees of separation from someone who can answer it or resolve it.

Is it possible that there's too little bureaucracy? A certain amount of structure can give employees confidence that they have a place and a role in a company. During the time I worked for Trader Joe's, it's very possible that I witnessed the company's transition from an admirably 'flat' organization to one with almost no organization at all.

☞ **Overall grade for 'No Bureaucracy'—B**
☞ **Contribution to brand**
   (Essential=5 Irrelevant=0)**—1**

☞ Value #5 - We are a national chain of neighborhood grocery stores

Trader Joe's makes a big deal of this claim, although much of its local flavor is window-dressing. During the Crew Members' indoctrination, the managers of my store explained that our neighborhood feel came from the large (crap) murals of Kansas City landmarks that were painted by a local (crap) artist.

There *are* some operational tactics that encourage customers to feel that they're in a local store. All the in-store signage is hand-drawn right in the store. Unlike other grocery chains that impose a 'planogram' — that is, where the head office tells store managers how and where products will be displayed — each Trader Joe's store makes its own merchandising decisions and thus each one looks a little different.

There's a massive amount of waste in a big grocery store. My store 'spoils' thousands of dollars' worth of food every day — food that would be destined for the dumpster. Our policy is to pull most foods off the shelves a day or two before their 'sell-by' dates, and produce is pulled off the displays as soon as it shows the first sign of overripeness, so most of that food is perfectly edible.

Although we have a donation program that gathers a lot of it and holds it for pickup by Kansas City food banks, the program is haphazard at best; if you just throw fifty loaves of bread in a garbage bag, and put that on the floor by the loading dock, and then pile another bag with fifty pounds of oranges on top of it, by the time the food bank comes to collect it, it's no longer too appetizing. Crew Members routinely throw truly rotten produce into bags with edible stuff, rendering the entire bag inedible. After Thanksgiving, we were left with dozens of turkeys that some food bank would surely have frozen and saved for Christmas. Instead, they went into the dumpster. The company is not particularly community-minded.

Notwithstanding the claim that individual store managers have complete operational control over their stores, you won't find managers stocking local items. For much of the summer, Missouri peaches, corn, and tomatoes are delicious; our store sold only produce that had been trucked from California, Arizona, or Mexico to Kansas City by way of Chicago. Sure, Trader Joe's stores in Maine sell lobster, but even McDonalds sells McLobster in Maine.

Store Captains are strictly warned off doing anything that attracts local press. Trader Joe's is conspicuously miserly when it comes to things like sponsoring neighborhood Little League teams. There's not even a means to send an email to your local store.

So, a neighborhood store? Not likely. It was precisely because Trader Joe's was *not* 'from here,' that it attracted a frenzied crowd of thousands during its Kansas City Grand Opening. (Ironically, my store is only a few blocks away from McGonigle's, which is an excellent, truly local family-run grocery.)

The one thing the company notes in the Crew Member Handbook that is relevant to the customer brand experience is, *"We want the customer's experience to be personal and intimate, like you would expect to find at a friendly, neighborhood store...such that the customer thinks of the store as 'their Trader Joe's.'"*

☞ **Overall grade for 'Neighborhood Feel' — C-/D+**

☞ **Contribution to brand**

    (Essential=5 Irrelevant=0) — **1.5**

☞ Value #6 - KAIZEN!

> *At Trader Joe's, Kaizen! is a way of life.*
> *Kaizen behavior simply means that every*
> *Crew Member at Trader Joe's is focused on*
> *achieving personal goals that contribute to*
> *the increasing success of the business. Every*
> *Crew Member strives to have continual,*
> *marginal improvement every day.*
> —Trader Joe's Crew Member Handbook

In the rest of the world, *'kaizen'* has a specific definition (look it up on Wikipedia, where there's a great entry on the subject). In summary, *kaizen* refers to continual process improvement. An essential aspect of *kaizen* is acknowledging, testing, and implementing good ideas from every employee. But, *kaizen* is not about an individual employee just 'having a great idea' and executing it. *Kaizen* is about testing new ideas according to scientific principles, and making statistically valid comparisons of results. An essential principle of *kaizen* is also that once a good idea is identified, it's actively propagated throughout the organization. That doesn't happen at Trader Joe's.

When we opened our store, I quickly realized that we were one of Kansas City's best shops for cheap-but-drinkable wines. While our $2.99 'Two-Buck Chuck' was—how can I put this—an acquired taste, our $5-$10 wines kicked ass compared to any other store in KC. In the first few weeks we were open, I met and traded tasting notes with several very knowledgeable local oenophiles who were eagerly buying and trying wines that they had never seen before.

I had the idea of inviting six or eight of these customers to a private wine-tasting party. We'd open a few bottles of wine. Each of them could make notes on them, and suggest a food pairing.

My little party idea would have made that group of customers—key influencers I'd already seen bringing *their* friends in to shop—feel appreciated. The notes and food suggestions would give our in-store artists something to write on signage, and comments could be attributed in a way that reinforced to other local customers that these were real, local, references. It would support the 'neighborhood store' value.

By that point, just a few weeks in, it was clear that my wine recommendations were appreciated by customers, because total strangers were coming into the store and asking for me by name, after being told about me by their friends. The order writer was upping the quantities on wines I'd tried and recommended.

Considering that the party was something I was planning on my own time and at my own expense, you'd think it was a no-brainer, at least to try. If it had worked—as I know it would have—the system would also be easy to roll out to other stores.

My suggestion was met with a blank stare, and then I was told, "We have our own way of doing wine tastings." Later on, we started doing them the Trader Joe's way. It involved serving tiny little slurps of the worst, usually sweetest, wines we stocked to random customers, dolloped out into the thimble-sized plastic cups that hospitals use to portion out pills.

It's perhaps telling that, at Trader Joe's, the word *'kaizen'* is written in all caps with an exclamation point. What we have isn't a word that describes a value; it's a word *instead* of a value. One of the traits that all cults have in common is, they don't take criticism well. You can't apply kaizen until you can admit that something you're doing can be improved.

☞ **Overall grade for *'kaizen'* — F**
☞ **Contribution to brand**
     (Essential=5 Irrelevant=0) — **0**

☞ Value #7 - The store is our Brand

The elucidation of this value in the Crew Member Handbook is so incoherent that I won't quote it in full, because I don't want to embarrass the company. (But seriously, what does, *"We will diligently act on [each customer's] behalf to satisfy their dreams related to our products and their experience"* mean? It reads like a sentence from the translated instructions you get when you buy an off-brand television with instructions translated from Malaysian.)

Look: the store is Trader Joe's brand almost by definition, at least in the sense that the company built its brand without using advertising to reach consumers where they live or work.

It's Trader Joe's brand in a much larger sense, which is that the incredible strength of the brand—its cult following—is created in the store. Remember how skeptical I was of Value #2 (We are a product driven company)? By ending the discussion of values by flatly saying, 'The store is our brand,' Dan Bane almost seems to be agreeing with me; it's not the products, it's the experience.

> *At Trader Joe's we recognize that our store is the personification of our Brand... Every store, every day and every Crew Member reflects the Trader Joe's brand. We must earn the customers' delight in our brand every time they shop with us.*
> —Trader Joe's Crew Member Handbook

As an ad guy, I wish I could tell you that attempting to build a brand without advertising is folly. Think of the most amazing brand campaigns—from Apple's classic '1984' to the re-branding of Old Spice— brilliant campaigns that influence[d] new customers to be favorably disposed towards a company or product and then to try it... Companies spend millions to get to that point where customers vote with their pocketbooks.

☞ **At the moment the customer has a real experience with your company or product—it doesn't matter how much money you spent on brand advertising. If the customer's direct experience with your company sucks, then you suck.** In fact, the more you spent, the higher the expectation you created, the angrier and more disappointed your new customer will be.

Part of the genius of Trader Joe's is that the company doesn't waste money on brand advertising and has never put itself at risk of creating dangerously raised expectations. Instead, it has invested in the customers' direct experience. ☞ **Gardiner's Fifth Law of Branding: The customer's experience trumps advertising any day.** I just read a corollary of that law on the Fast Company web site, where one of their bloggers wrote, 'Culture Eats Strategy For Lunch.'

Strategic brand advertising is about putting your customer in a favorable frame of mind, but it is, at best, a fragile frame of mind. Trader Joe's approach, in which the cultural brand is built by the very employees who meet your customers face-to-face every day, creates customers who are willing to cut you some slack. They'll keep coming back, and give you a second (and third, and fourth...) chance.

☞ **Overall grade for 'Store-as-brand' — A**

☞ **Contribution to brand**

(Essential=5 Irrelevant=0) **— 5**

☞ The Mission Statement

Only the most tenacious of readers of the Trader Joe's Member Handbook will be able to divine the company's mission statement. It's buried in an appendix to the handbook, and not even listed in the Table of Contents. That's noteworthy in itself, because most modern businesses make a big deal of their 'Mission.' They should, anyway, because most modern companies have paid big bucks to some bullshit consultant to help write it. Maybe companies like Trader Joe's *that really believe they're on a mission* don't pay much attention to writing it down.

Nonetheless, there are two 'letters' from current CEO Dan Bane at the back of the handbook, and in one of them he states...

> *The mission of Trader Joe's is to give our customers the best food and beverage values that they can find anywhere and to provide them with the information required for informed buying decisions.*

We provide these with...a sense of warmth, friendliness, fun, individual pride and company spirit.

We set trends. We lead our customers rather than following them.

We view ourselves as the purchasing agent of food and beverages for intelligent, educated, inquisitive individuals.

Later in the same letter, Bane describes Trader Joe's target customers as intelligent and well educated; he claims they're interested in new ideas; they travel; they're value-oriented and health-conscious.

In the time that I worked for the company, I never saw any actual research done, so I cannot attest to the quality of data those claims are based on. Trader Joe's says that 80% of its customers have some college education; matching that 'statistic' against U.S. census data leads to the conclusion that the chain's clientele is about 1.5 times as likely to have attended college as the U.S. population overall.

Based on direct experience in my store, I'd say the clientele is, at best, slightly more sophisticated and diverse than that of the average grocery store in the suburban Midwest. Most people seemed satisfied, or even very satisfied, with Trader Joe's prices. As for being health conscious, it was definitely true that our store siphoned off customers from the nearby Whole Foods store. Trader Joe's prices on organics—when we offered them—were cheaper than 'Whole Paycheck.'

Many people seemed aware of Trader Joe's claim that virtually none of the food sold in the store included artificial colors or preservatives, but few seemed to have carefully read the labels. Most Trader Joe's prepared foods are loaded with salt, and the company's definition of a 'serving size' and the attendant calorie counts are every bit as disingenuous as those of the food industry as a whole.

At the end of the second rambling letter, Bane concludes...

> *Why do they shop at Trader Joe's?*
>
> *Our people are warm and friendly.*
> *It's fun and an adventure.*
> *They find unexpected products.*
> *They experience cheap thrills.*
> *Our people are helpful and knowledgeable.*
> *They know that we have tested each product*
> *to ensure quality and satisfaction.*
> *They trust us.*

How does that list match my own direct experience?

"Warm and friendly"? That's a yes.

"Fun," yes.

"Adventure" is a stretch. Yes, they make unexpected finds, but they often look for something they loved last week, but which is out of stock this week.

"Cheap thrills" is another stretch.

Our people are helpful, but *knowledgeable*? Not so much. One of the managers in my store, who wrote the order for the frozen section where we stocked two products called Cod Provençale and Polenta Provençale, pronounced the word 'Provençale' like 'proven kale.' Since I was known to be something of an amateur chef, a young employee once turned to me for expert advice, asking, "How do you make a tuna salad sandwich?"

What I'm saying is, neither the Hawaiian Shirts nor the Crew Members are typically real epicures.

I doubt most customers are particularly impressed with Trader Joe's testing procedures, but I do know that they trust the company.

Bane signs off with this observation...

> *You're going to have to be a special person to*
> *make sure that when every customer leaves*
> *the store they think to themselves, "That was*

fun and I got a good deal." When that happens no one can touch us.

☞ **Overall grade for Mission — C**
☞ **Contribution to brand**
(Essential=5 Irrelevant=0) — **2**

☞ Things we don't do, that make us different, according to Trader Joe's

After the discussion of those values in the Crew Member Handbook, there's *'A Message to All Trader Joe's Crewmembers'* that also appears over Bane's signature.

Bane's description of what makes the company different from other grocers begins with a long list of things Trader Joe's *isn't*, and things it doesn't do. This list includes a few flat statements that are at best arguable, like this one: *"[We don't] have big stores— Big stores cost too much."*

While I suppose it's a truism that big stores cost more than small ones, there is such a thing as efficiency of scale. That's presumably why, although the average Trader Joe's store is very small compared to other supermarkets, the size of new Trader Joe's stores has approximately doubled during the time Bane's been the CEO. (And the idea that big stores can't be cost effective will come as a surprise to Costco.)

Bane notes that Trader Joe's doesn't use an ad agency. *"We write the Fearless Flyer and radio spots ourselves."* Any ad professional who sees Trader Joe's marketing materials will not be surprised to learn the company writes its own stuff. What can I say about the Fearless Flyer? I guess that it's the work of spirited amateurs.

Another expense Trader Joe's eschews is a public relations firm. *"They are a waste of money,"* Bane says. *"If you give your customers great products at great prices, why do you need one?"*

Bane's at least half-right about PR ☞ **When you run one of the most secretive companies in America, and never cooperate with journalists, a PR firm is certainly a waste of money.**

The handbook makes a point that Trader Joe's doesn't franchise. The 'explanation' for this is that the company wants to retain control over its people, products, prices, and level of personalized service. Either Trader Joe's misrepresents the famous autonomy of Store Captains, or the head office in Monrovia exerts less control over its stores than most franchisors. (The emphasis on personalized service, though, betrays the significance of *that* factor.)

"[We don't] have cold, mechanical employees" is another claim. And, to Trader Joe's credit, they don't.

"[We don't] appeal to broad consumer markets—Our customers are unique." This is another Trader Joe's claim that is simultaneously wrongheaded and insightful. My store in Kansas City serves a racially and socioeconomically diverse population that reflects the cross section of the people living within a few miles of the store. That only makes sense; you don't sell eight billion dollars' worth of stuff without appealing to a broad market. ☞ **What all those people really have in common is, they *like to be treated* individually.**

•

☞ **And last but not least, a few more things we do, that make us different, according to Trader Joe's...**

☞ *"1. Intensive buying."*
"I believe that our approach to buying at Trader Joe's is unique," Bane writes. *"I refer to it as intensive buying."*

The life of a Trader Joe's buyer may well be intense. And it's certainly true that the way Trader Joe's conducts its business in general (i.e., paying for everything out of cash on hand) and the way it operates as a grocery store (i.e., not charging slotting allowances for the few 'name brand' products it carries) is unique.

But.

There's nothing in Bane's description of the *buying process* that would seem particularly unique to a buyer from, say, Whole Foods. Our buyers travel the world; their buyers travel the world. We subject new

116

products to tasting panels; they have tasting panels, too. We make decisions quickly to prevent our competitors from getting new products first... Blah, blah, blan.

If Dan Bane really believes that his buyers, and the procedures they follow to acquire new products, are the #1 thing that Trader Joe's does to differentiate itself from competitors, it can only be because he really believes in the so-called 'value' of being a product-driven company.

It's not the first time I've found a CEO who doesn't really know why his company's succeeding.

☞ *"2. Providing Information to our Customers"*

"We believe that there is a segment of the population who wants to make their own decisions to buy based on information," Bane says. *"These are intelligent customers. Notice, I didn't say consumer. We never use that word at Trader Joe's. A customer is an individual. A consumer crams down garbage."*
—Trader Joe's Crew Member Handbook

Gosh, that will come as a disappointment to 'Consumer Reports,' but look on the bright side: it takes all the pressure off the Consumer Protection Agency. But seriously, folks, Trader Joe's calls itself *"an informative retailer...like L.L. Bean."*

Trader Joe's grocery flyers and most of the company's product labels, have higher-than-average word counts. ☞ **It's one of the few remaining companies willing to give its customers (not consumers!) credit for being able to read.** As for the quality of that information, well, it ain't Cook's Illustrated.

Trader Joe's claims, *"[W]e strongly believe that knowledgeable employees are essential for an informative retailer. Each of our stores has a special expense account to allow our people to sample our products, and we encourage you to try everything."*

There are great grocery chains, like Wegman's in New York State, that really strive to put food experts on the grocery store floor where they can advise and interact with customers. Wegman's routinely sends ordinary retail employees to spend time with the people who produce the foods they sell. Even my local Costco, here in Kansas City, has a trained sommelier in the wine department. Trader Joe's doesn't do that. Once a year, it picks a handful of senior Store Captains and those people go to Italy with one of the buyers. But it's a perk, not training.

One of Trader Joe's charms is the way all the signage in the store is hand-drawn by in-store sign artists. It's telling that while each store recruits one or more 'real' artists to fill this specialized role—my store hired two or three grads from the highly regarded Kansas City Art Institute—there's no parallel role for a local copywriter or foodie. That can make for some accidentally hilarious signage.

At my store, we had a sign artist who seemed to delight in using the French expression *'Sacre bleu!'* as a headline. The thing is, French is spoken in deeply Catholic countries, where *Sacre bleu* is a profane expression. While it literally means 'blue host,' an accurate contextual translation would be quite different. Imagine walking through a French public market, and coming across a handwritten sign proclaiming, in English:

Holy Shit!
Red Peppers
89 cents

☞ "3. A Completely Satisfying Shopping Experience for our Customers"

By now, you're probably wondering when, if ever, I'll agree with Trader Joe's about what makes customers love the store. Well, with this point, Bane's on the money.

"Why do they shop at Trader Joe's?" he asks, and the first point he makes in answering the question is, *"Our people are warm and friendly."*

"You're going to have to be a special person to make sure that when every customer leaves the store," Bane writes, *"they think to themselves, 'That was fun, and I got a good deal.' When that happens no one can touch us."*

The Secret

☞ *Parsing the real reasons for the success of Trader Joe's cultural brand*

[Author's note: Having read this far, you've got an appreciation for the experience and perspective that I brought to Trader Joe's. You should also have a sense of just how true Trader Joe's is to its own stated values, and how relevant those things are to the brand. After the better part of a year on the floor at Trader Joe's, I've come to the conclusion that The Secret of Trader Joe's devoted brand following is so simple that, for my entire career in advertising, it was hiding in plain sight, right in front of me. In some ways, it's so obvious that if I just blurt it out, you might think it couldn't really be *The* Secret. Instead, in the third part of this book, I'll parse all that I learned about the company's values, and hope that you, too, will come to the same conclusion.]

Value #1 is Integrity. Trader Joe's integrity is just OK when seen from the perspective of suppliers, labor rights groups, and environmentalists. ☞ **It's solid when seen from the perspective of the customer.**

Value #2 is 'We are a product driven Company.' Although there are strengths and weaknesses across Trader Joe's offerings, strengths prevail. Most products are of reasonable-to-good quality at good-to-very-good prices. ☞ **They're good *enough*.** But there's no explanation for the fact that Trader Joe's strongest market, Manhattan, is precisely the market where the store's offerings are the most mundane by comparison to local rivals.

Value #3 is that good ol' WOW customer experience. *The New Yorker's* Patricia Marx came dangerously close to scooping me when she noted that the products were not that special, but that the staff were conspicuously friendly. ☞ **The anonymous friend Marx quotes, who described Trader Joe's as 'the**

home of lonely food,' actually did scoop me. *She gets it.*

'No Bureaucracy' is Value #4. It's relevant insofar as every Crew Member is empowered to solve your problem, or at least take you straight to someone who can solve it, whatever it might be.

As for Value #5, the idea that Trader Joe's is 'a national chain of neighborhood grocery stores,' I've shown you that's a largely unsupported claim. But, the Crew Member Handbook is right for the wrong reasons when, in the discussion of this value, it claims that ☞ *"Each store...is operated such that the customer thinks of the store as their Trader Joe's."*

Value #6 is, supposedly, KAIZEN! (God, I'm happy to have typed that word, Trader Joe's style, in all caps with an exclamation point, for the last time.) *Kaizen*? Not likely. See the appendix titled 'Gardiner's Paradox,' and you'll realize that, if anything, Trader Joe's is determined *not* to improve

most of the things that make it its wonderful,
inefficient self.

Value #7 is, 'The store is our Brand.' The company's
own elaboration of this notion is almost gibberish,
but the take-away you need is that ☞ **the brand
experience happens in the store** (not,
conspicuously, downstream from the store in your
kitchen or at your table, which would be the key
brand experience if, as Trader Joe's claims, it was
mainly about the *products*). That is one of the keys to
The Secret.

Two of the "don'ts" that Trader Joe's brags about are,
we don't have an ad agency and we don't have a PR
firm, so brand expectations are definitely not set
upstream from the store.

Two more "don'ts" are the last two pieces of
evidence you need to crack The Secret. We don't
have cold, mechanical employees, and we don't
think of our customers as a "broad consumer
market." We think of them as unique individuals.

☞ **Those are the same traits that define the relationship you have with your friends**

Integrity: You don't insist that your friends behave with perfect integrity everywhere in their lives—if you did, you wouldn't have many friends. ☞ **All you insist is that they behave with integrity towards you**, and that if they have a failing in that regard, they acknowledge it and apologize.

Products: ☞ **You don't define your friends by the things they have, or what you get from them; what's important is your friends'** *intentions* **towards you.** When a friend gives you something, you tend to evaluate it from a positive perspective, at least initially. Of course, eventually if you feel that the friendship is all one way, and that you're contributing more than the value you get from the friendship in return, you'll drop away.

That brings us to the 'wow' factor. (Again, now that I've finally reached the end of this book and I'm about to forsake Crew Member status, I'll stop typing 'wow' in all caps.)

That New Yorker's take on it—that it's a store full of lonely food—really provides an insight into the *esprit de corps* between customers and staff at Trader Joe's. People talk to each other. Just the other day, my wife was shopping in what we call the 'HABA' aisle (it stands for 'health and beauty aids') when a total stranger started a long conversation about the oatmeal soap.

That's just not the kind of thing that happens in regular grocery stores. Where *do* people comfortably initiate conversations with strangers? At a party; you do it in places where you think, I might not know this person, but if ☞ **they're a friend of my friend,** they can't be all bad... There's even a couple of blogs devoted to spottings of cute Trader Joe's Crew Members. (I've never been mentioned on it, but I'm not bitter.)

In the neighborhood: Our customers think of Trader Joe's as 'their store' because of the one-to-one interactions they have with Crew Members and other customers on the floor of the store. (Which, according to Value #7, is our brand.) The interactions customers have on the floor are warm and genuine.
☞ **They know that their friends see them for who they are, as an individual, and like any friendship, that goes both ways.**

●

I worked at Trader Joe's for quite a while before it occurred to me that in my career in advertising, I'd conceived ads and built brands motivated by consumers' greed, vanity, egos, fears, sense of insecurity, and (of course) sex drives. I presented brands as comfortable, familiar, and trusted; sure. ☞ **But I have never, ever, been asked to write an ad in which the brand attribute was, "We are your friends."**

●●

☞ **A feeling of shared friendship. That's Trader Joe's branding secret.** Millions of people shop at Trader Joe's because they believe—based on millions of face-to-face interactions with Crew Members, that Trader Joe's, the people who work there, and even other customers are *their friends*.

●●●

You can create a killer ad campaign for a great new product, sell it for a sharp price, even back it with a strict guarantee...but if the customer's direct experience of the transaction makes him think, "These people are assholes," the customer won't like it, won't recommend you, and won't come back. ☞ **You can get everything else right, and if the customer doesn't like you, you'll sell to them once, at most.**

Once you forge that bond of friendship between the customer and your brand, everything changes. ☞ **If the customer likes you, you can get everything**

else wrong, and they'll give you multiple chances to make it right.

Remember, back under the heading of Value #2, I invoked Clayton Christensen's observation that a customer who buys a 1/4" drill bit doesn't want a drill bit, he wants a 1/4" hole? Then, I extrapolated that to a typical Trader Joe's customer with an entire cart of purchases, who's hired those groceries to provide quick, convenient, at-home, single-serving meals.

☞ **What if we extrapolate still further and ask, "What does a Trader Joe's shopper expect the *brand* to provide?"** i.e., what makes a Trader Joe's shopper choose Trader Joe's for those prepared meals over another store?

The answer is: the thing our shoppers can *only* get at our store. ☞ **The thing they can only get at Trader Joe's is *a few minutes among friends who'll accept them as they are*.**

If that sounds a little too New Age-y for ya', consider this sobering statistic: Since the founding of Trader Joe's, the percentage of the population who live alone has doubled. In the last ten years—a period in which Trader Joe's sales have approximately doubled —the percentage of single-person households has increased about 50%. According to the U.S. Census Bureau, the district with the largest percentage of single-person households is...Manhattan. Yes, the home of Trader Joe's #1 and #2 stores. The place where *The New Yorker* magazine's reporter remarked that the produce wasn't so special, but the staff was sure friendly.

And, at the risk of stating the obvious, the rise of Trader Joe's also coincides with ubiquitous new media and communication technologies, from email and texting to Twitter and Facebook, that nominally 'connect' us while we actually withdraw into technological cocoons. ☞ **The fact that we spend hours a day 'socializing' with our phones and computers increases the value of the face-to-face social interactions we experience at Trader Joe's.**

I rest my case.

••••

I paid ten bucks for this book, you're thinking, *and all he tells me is, I need to make my customers like me. How the hell do I do that?*

Ah, that's The Secret. ☞ **You make your customers think of you as their friend... By. Being. Their. Friend.**

At Trader Joe's, Crew Members are brand surrogates. Because it's a labor-intensive retail setting, there are millions of opportunities for face-to-face interactions. But creating friendships isn't specifically dependent on face time *per se.* The necessary and sufficient condition is that ☞ **interactions—whether they happen in person, on the phone, via email, text message, or web chat— are individual and authentic.**

Strategic brands are built on claims. McDonalds put apple slices and a yogurt dip on the menu, and claimed that it had your health in mind (knowing all the while that parents would see the billboard for apple dippers, and pull into the drive-through thinking, McDonalds isn't so bad, and then the kids would throw a tantrum to get the fries anyway).

Cultural brands are not based on mere claims; they take authenticity. Patagonia's environmentally-driven brand is built on its willingness to submit itself to the closest scrutiny of its actions. ☞ **Actions trump claims.**

Trader Joe's great cultural brand certainly can't stand up to such scrutiny where its actions and products are concerned, but it doesn't have to; it's not built on claims or actions, but rather on intention. Many Crew Members really do want to make your day. We may not always succeed, but that's the beauty of 'friending' (sorry Facebook) instead of conventional branding. ☞ **You don't choose your friends based on what they do to you or for you; you choose** them based on what they try to do, what you believe they would do in a pinch, what they want, wish, and hope for on your behalf.

☞ Between friends, intentions are even more powerful than actions.

Four steps to building a brand like Trader Joe's

☞ Get enough people

☞ Get the right people

☞ Empower them

☞ Don't completely fuck up everything else

☞ **The first step to building an outstanding relationship between your customers and your staff is the easiest one to implement: All it takes is more staff.** Zeynep Tom, a professor at M.I.T., studied Trader Joe's and several other low-cost retailers that, paradoxically, had high labor costs; they had more workers per square foot in their stores and paid them higher than average salaries in the retail sector. He learned that stores with more, better-paid staff have higher sales per square foot and per employee than stores that try to cut customer service costs.

As James Surowiecki noted in *The New Yorker* magazine, "When Bob Nardelli took over Home Depot, in 2000, he reduced the number of salespeople on the floor and turned many full-time jobs into part-time ones... The company's customer-service ratings plummeted, and its sales growth stalled." In 2007, Circuit City decided to cut customer-service costs by firing thousands of senior salespeople and replacing them with newbies they could pay less. The company was bankrupt a few years later.

The benefit of more staff, and the direct connection between customer service interaction and brand equity is, perhaps, most obvious in a retail setting, but it's not limited to retail. How often have you been lost in an interminable telephone menu seeking information, advice, or tech support? Press 1 if you never want to do business with that company again.

If the math on this is so simple, why do so many companies get it wrong? Probably because the returns on investment in customer service staff are hard to put your finger on, but the cost-savings associated with staff reductions are immediate and quantifiable.

Remember when, way back at the beginning of this book, I made the case that retail—and especially grocery—was the perfect branding laboratory? The result of Trader Joe's great branding experiment will transfer to your business, even if you're not a grocer or a retailer. ☞ **Every transaction, whether it's retail, B2C, B2B; online or face-to-face; a one-time purchase or a long-term relationship...every transaction comes down to an interaction between people.** (When you're in that interminable phone menu, you're not mad at the phone, you're mad at the *person* who decided a phone system would be more efficient than a receptionist.)

If you're not a grocer—and I hope most of my readers aren't—what you need to do is look at your business and figure out who's selling and who's buying. Flood the seller zone with people who really, really want to make those buyers happy.

☞ **Look at anything that constitutes a layer between the sellers and buyers, and figure out how you can make that layer a medium for personal communication.** If it can't be personalized, remove it.

The second step is to get the right people. Trader Joe's has learned that paying starting salaries of around $12.50 an hour (and offering benefits to workers who put in as few as 20 hours per month) is enough to get the company its pick of workers. Part of that is probably a 'benefit' of an economy that's been persistently weak for the American middle class for years.

Trader Joe's also extracts a ton of value from one of America's least-utilized natural resources: the pool of artsy, creative, college-educated young people who graduate without the hard skills that would allow them to get technical jobs. As it turns out, kids who graduated from their local college theater program and (surprise!) couldn't get a job acting; kids who got their bachelor's degree in history and then realized (oops!) there aren't too many job openings for historians...lots of those kids make great customer-service employees.

☞ **If you want to build a brand like Trader Joe's, you can spend less time and money recruiting for highly sought-after hard skills, and more emphasis on the softest skill of all: empathy.** Hire those empathetic souls, and motivating them won't be problem because they'll provide great customer service and turn your customers into friends just by being themselves.

Those kids especially show their value in an environment where they're empowered to do whatever it takes to make sure customers are happy, and they're given some creative leeway. Many of them come to work at Trader Joe's and feel really appreciated and (bonus!) that coming to work is almost an extension of their social life, because they're surrounded by people like themselves.

When coming to work is kind of fun, and when the customers you deal with think your job is kind of cool, interactions between staff and customers are reinforced in a virtuous cycle. In my job at Trader Joe's, I've dealt with thousands of customers. I've encountered a few real assholes; that's inevitable. But I genuinely like most of them.

Remember that cashier from Megafoods? The one who, when asked how she was, said, "I'll be fine in 45 minutes, when I get off work."

What she was really telling you was, "You may think this is a great store, but the people who know the business best, the employees, think it sucks to be here."

That's not an answer you'll hear very often at Trader Joe's. When the people who come up to your cash register break into a genuine smile when they see you, and when it seems that they really want to know how you are when they're asking, it's hard to be in a bad mood.

Ask yourself what businesses you really like to frequent and I bet that one thing they have in common is that the employees seem to be having a good time.

☞ **The third step, now that you've determined to put enough people on this brand-building assignment, and you've found the right kind of people for this assignment is empowering them to fulfill their mission.**

As a company, you have to be totally committed to creating an authentic 'wow' experience. There's not an algorithm for wow; it's not behavior you can program, or something you can train people to deliver. Because it's (usually) the result of an encounter between individuals—it could be face-to-face but it can just as easily happen over the phone, or by email, chat, whatever—what you're encouraging is your employees to just be their individual selves.

It would be easy to send a memo to that effect, but remember Surfing Lesson #4, about committing to the wave? As a company, you need to commit to empowering your employees to doing what it takes to satisfy your customers. That means following Trader Joe's example. ☞ **Make sure that everyone knows that they'll be rewarded, not punished, if they take the time to create that 'wow' experience, no matter how many other assignments or duties they've got.**

If you're thinking, *I'll create a cadre of empathetic customer service people who'll befriend my customers and deliver 'wow' experiences,* you're learning the wrong lesson here. You *do* want to do that, but that's not all you want to do. It works for Trader Joe's because it's *everyone's* responsibility, all the time.

Hiring enough staff, hiring the right staff, and empowering them may—I guess I have to admit, will —mean your labor costs will go up when you attempt to build a brand like Trader Joe's. The proof that this approach is cost-effective is simply that Theo Albrecht didn't make a single change to Joe Coulombe's branding methodology in the 30+ years he owned the business. Walk through any Aldi store and you'll know that Albrecht doesn't waste any money.

As an 'ad guy,' I hate to admit that the logical place to find that budget is in the money that you now spend on marketing, PR, and advertising. ☞ **The best thing about building a brand like Trader Joe's is that you only have to do it once.** You know Burberry's? Twenty years ago, the maker of high-end British woolens had a great reputation...among grandmothers. They looked at their brand and realized it was dying; *literally* dying, all their customers were that old. Burberry's had to redesign its entire line, get Kate Moss out of rehab, and spend a fortune to reposition itself for an audience of entitled trust-fund babies (who are notoriously fickle, and will no doubt drop it again, anyway).

GM spent decades positioning Cadillac as the quintessential American land yacht, only to find, some time around 1990, that everyone who could afford a luxury car suddenly wanted a European performance sedan like a BMW or Mercedes. Cadillac had to retool its entire line—and enter the 24 hours of Le Mans, for God's sake—to convince a new generation of buyers that its cars were *not* land yachts.

McDonalds, after years of pushing Happy Meals as the gateway to a Supersized adulthood, now finds itself on the defensive; it's the *piñata* for America's obesity epidemic, and basically committed to spending a fortune to put out this message: *We're not killing your kids*.

That's never, ever going to happen to you if you build your brand like Trader Joe's, because having people genuinely like you; having people just want to come to your place and hang out with you; having people curious about what you'll get up to next, because *you're their friend*...those are things that are never going to go out of style.

☞ **The fourth step is, don't completely fuck up everything else.**

In some ways, the better the job your ad agency did building a great strategic brand for your company, the harder you had to work: Great ads just raise customer expectations. When customers walk into Trader Joe's and think, "Ah, here I am at my friends' store," they expect to have fun, buy stuff that's good enough, and leave with their self-respect. *There's a difference between high expectations and raised ones;* it's the difference between going to a good restaurant with your best friend, or going to a great restaurant with a Michelin star and eating alone. While you're more likely to leave the first restaurant happy and satisfied, even if the second restaurant turned out great, it's likely that you approached it much more critically.

The beauty of building a brand like Trader Joe's is that if your customers genuinely like you — not your products, but *you* — they'll cut you plenty of slack. As I noted earlier, you can get everything else right, and if your customers think you're an asshole, they'll never come back. ☞ **If they like you, you can get almost everything wrong and, at the very least, they'll give you another chance.**

OK. Now you know how Trader Joe's cultural brand was built, and you want to build one like it. How can you decide what 'good enough' means, when it comes to the product or service you deliver?

☞ **Ask yourself, "Is this what I'd do for my friend; is it what I'd expect *from* a friend?"**

If the answer is *yes*, you're on your way. You don't even need to read the rest of this book. But if you do plan to follow my advice, you can read three appendices, in which I'll outline a few pitfalls you'll encounter along the way, and—possibly—show you how Trader Joe's itself is veering off course.

Good luck.

Three Dilemmas

If you've read this far, you've probably been at least
somewhat convinced by my thesis—that you can
build a vibrant, valuable brand with culture just as
easily as you can with strategy. You may be poised to
emulate Trader Joe's, and create a great brand of
your own, without spending a cent on advertising.

Be warned: In the paragraph above, I wrote "just as
easily" and not *just* 'easily.' Building your brand on a
foundation of corporate culture is easy to understand;
it doesn't take a big ad budget. It does, however, take
work, a disciplined focus, and a long-term faith in
your employees, because unlike old-fashioned
strategic branding, there are few metrics for culture.

If you set out to build your brand at the interface of
your customer and your customer service (it's

literally an interface; something often done face-to-face) at some point you're going to confront a few dilemmas.

☞ **The first dilemma is that there's a fine line between 'culture' and 'cult.'**

Trader Joe's founder Joe Coulombe once told a writer from *Fortune* that, "The Albrechts may own the store, but I still own the cult." He was laughing as he said it, but like many jokes, there's an element of truth to it.

☞ **Criticism—even productive criticism—is never welcome in a cult.** At Trader Joe's, many of the employees are aghast at the amount of salt in the company's prepared foods, at excessive packaging, and at the carbon footprint of products like naan bread that's made and frozen in India and shipped frozen to stores in the U.S. And yet, while employees talk about those issues amongst themselves, there's a clear sense that it would be a career-limiting move to mention them to visiting dignitaries from the regional or head office.

It's not just on the slippery decks at Trader Joe's where the slide from culture to cult's a risk. Look at Apple: Remember the scary, heavy handed way it dealt with the tech blogger who found a prototype iPhone in a Silicon Valley bar? It's clear, too, that no one at Apple has ever dared to point out that hiding the fucking on/off switch on iMacs is just stupid. And you can be sure that it's a career-limiting move in Cupertino to point out that Apple's packaging raises wastefulness to an art form.

If I could offer you an easy way to build an enthusiastic culture while avoiding the risk of becoming a self-congratulatory cult, I would do so. But then, it would not be a real dilemma, would it? You're just going to have to deal with it. At least I warned you.

☞ **The second dilemma is that the practices that build cultural brands produce systems that are easy for employees to game.**

Many companies have protocols that ensure customer service staff that are nominally polite (rules like, "Always greet the customer," or say, "Thank you. Come again.") Some go further and strive to create a clearly defined corporate culture—to build their brands from the inside—but the stronger the culture (or the cult) the easier it is for employees to co-opt the language of that culture, adopt the tropes of that culture, and to game the system.

An example: *"What do the bells mean?"* is the most common question I get from customers.

☞ **One bell means, there's a line at the cash registers**

☞ **Two bells mean a cashier needs general assistance**

☞ **Three bells mean a manager is needed**

Since the bells are rung at the cash registers, there's always a Hawaiian Shirt nearby. Responding to bells is a 'reviewed' aspect of job performance; the idea is to respond quickly while calling out 'Two bells!' so that the rest of the staff know you've got dibs on that customer. Then, you run over and find out what's up. 'Two bells' are usually rung because a customer needs a carryout or some other kind of help.

Trader Joe's wants its brand to be fun, enthusiastic, and entertaining—so some employees respond to bells with wildly exaggerated shouts of 'Two bells!' using strange intonations or making an exaggerated show of running to respond—to a degree that nearby customers are actually alarmed. This kind of histrionic response earns you a positive note on your review, while making a great, meaningful, but quiet connection with a customer probably goes unnoticed.

Some of your employees will game the system consciously to get a good review and others will do it unconsciously.

☞ **What's actually valuable in your brand's relationship with customers is sincerity,** but your managers are not polygraph operators. Likewise, genuine enthusiasm is always welcome, but when customers start to feel that it's just an act, it's merely infuriating.

The over-friendliness of some Trader Joc's Crew Members is one of the most-often cited irritants by our shoppers. It's even come up in a TED lecture by MIT prof Sherry Turkle. The snarky blog 'Fucked in Park Slope' put up a post on the subject that triggered over 50 comments, including, *"I just don't like the play-by-play Howard Cosell, 'What, ANOTHER bag of frozen blueberries, WOW' kind of commentary, by someone who is ringing up my groceries."*

Another commenter added, *"I'm just not sure what sort of Walt-Disney-themed corporate training that the cashiers are put through to become so obnoxiously involved with their customers at check-out. I'm all for a smile or two, but these people just take it way too far."*

Again, I wish I had an easy answer for you on this, but if I did, it wouldn't be a real dilemma. Just because culture's hard to evaluate doesn't mean you shouldn't try to create it in your own company. It's worked for Trader Joe's.

☞ **The third dilemma is that building your brand by befriending your customer is both the ultimate 'soft' branding idea and ultimately dependent on your front-line employees.**

At many businesses, the brand is the company's most valuable single asset; it can be worth more than all the real estate, inventory, or tooling. As you would expect, most businesses place responsibility for the brand in the hands of one of their most highly paid employees—someone with a title like, Vice-president, Marketing.

If you follow my advice, your valuable brand will be taken out of the hands of that highly paid VP and placed in the hands of your lowest-paid employees.

That idea may scare you, but there's no logical basis for your fears. You may have already spent a fortune building your brand the old-fashioned way, and your great ads may indeed drive millions of customers into your store, but shitty customer service will always prevent you from getting a return on that brand investment. ☞ **Your lowest-paid employees have always been empowered to *erode* brand value; why not empower them to create it?**

> [Author's Note: My friend Harry summarizes it thusly: Your challenge is to turn that Megafoods "I'll be fine when I'm outta this dump" cashier into a Trader Joe's "I'm diggin' this bee-yootiful day and may I be so bold as to say that you have a lovely pair of cantaloupes" Crew Member—Harry gets it, but try to execute it in a way that won't get people slapped, eh?]

Gardiner's Paradox

Although much of this book describes the daily chaos of life in Trader Joe's, until you've been a Crew Member for a few months you can't fully grasp what it's like. (It's not something we really let customers see.)

Most days, Crew Members bounce along in an existence that is sort of a fractal pattern of crisis. At the smallest level, it's a customer who knocks a bottle of wine off a display, causing the nearest Crew Member to leave a teetering stack of five cases of wine in the middle of the sales floor while he races into the back room to get the 'Zamboni' — a wheeled wet-vac we use to suck up spills, only to find that the holding tank's already full from a previous spill. Pull back a little further, and you'll see the store run out of potato chips on a Saturday afternoon during football season, when everyone's stocking up on snacks for tomorrow afternoon. Or the truck loaded with a huge wine delivery before New Year's Eve delayed for hours in a blizzard.

One recurring problem is that Crew Members often simply forget when they are supposed to work, because the scheduling system is chaotic, too. There is no discernible pattern to Crew Members' days off, and it's common to be scheduled for a different start time every day of the week. Crew Members check the schedule by flipping through a binder in the store, finding their names on a spreadsheet, and reading across it while scribbling the next week's start times on a Post-It Note, usually looking over someone else's shoulder at the crowded 'pit' (where the manager sits looking out over the store). It's easy to get it wrong.

If it seems to you, the casual reader, that systems could be put in place to minimize these problems, you can imagine how baffled I was working for the company.

There doesn't seem to be any effort to capture data or build predictive models of consumer demand for key products; that's done entirely by the seat of the order writer's pants, and if the order is adjusted by a manager, *that* decision is also based on instinct and experience — which are great things in business, but not substitutes for actual knowledge.

Through our first midwestern winter, my store's managers were surprised every time the truck from Chicago was delayed by the weather. Here's a note from the Dept. of Things You Should Already Know: when your warehouse is in a city that is also home to one of the National Hockey League's 'original six' teams, you should expect snow in the winter.

I'll never understand why Crew Members can't check their schedules from home. Each store prepares its schedule on the store's computer system, which is linked to the head office system; there's already a password-protected, employee-only area of the company web site. In a few hours, any computer programmer worth his salt could create a system that would make it possible for Crew Members to check their schedule online.

Really, aren't *all* these little problems the kind of things that good managers—up and down the company org chart—could devise systems to eliminate, or at least mitigate? I was mulling all this over one day in the store, when suddenly something hit me. No, not a teetering stack of five cases of wine, but something I call ☞ **Gardiner's Paradox.**

The business of Trader Joe's is, at its core, very simple: getting stuff off the truck, onto the shelf, then out the door. Every one of those steps is manual. The challenge is just handling all that stuff, in the midst of that day-to-day chaos.

Some Crew Members are lifesavers: They thrive on chaos, and in spite of any number of distractions can 'throw' and face an entire shelf at manic speed, in between wine spills and before it's time for them to return to the cash register where they'll scan and bag customers' groceries so fast their hands blur.

Those Crew Members don't waste time complaining about recurring problems or questioning the wisdom of their managers. They just work that much faster. Imagine someone playing a cross between the old-school video game Tetris and the fairground game Whack-a-Mole.

☞ **Paradoxically, by hiring and promoting those employees who thrive while operating like that for hours at a time, Trader Joe's reinforces chaos,** because it's hiring and promoting the people least likely to impose order on the system. Why *would* those hyperactive, chaos-loving Crew Members solve those recurring problems? Bringing order and efficiency to the store's day-to-day operations would eliminate the situations in which they shine and are most valuable to the enterprise.

☞ **Who *would* solve those problems? Someone who hates chaos. Someone who's driven crazy by**

it. Someone, ironically, who would be a miserable Crew Member.

Every business has a fundamental problem (or at most a handful of them). And every business is tempted to look for employees who can work around that problem, rather than employees who will solve it.

Is the good ship Trader Joe's changing course?

The eight months that I spent as a Trader Joe's Crew Member were, in hindsight, possibly the last time the company really applied the principles I've described in this book. As I've noted, the current management doesn't appear to fully understand why Joe Coulombe's '60s-era corporate culture continued to yield tremendous brand equity during the period of explosive growth *after* his departure.

Even without the original Joe, Trader Joe's culture stayed consistent for a long time. The company's second CEO, John Shields, wasn't a grocer but he was still a 'retail guy.' Besides, the company was owned by Theo Albrecht who was himself a second-generation grocer and the founder of a German grocery chain, Aldi, which has much in common with Trader Joe's. (There are even a few Trader Joe's products sold in Aldi stores in Germany.)

While Theo Albrecht was alive, I'm sure he vetoed any significant cultural changes to a business that had proven to be one of the best investments of the century.

Trader Joe's is only on its third CEO. The current one, Dan Bane, is an ex-accountant. As I noted in the previous chapter, it's notoriously difficult to assign numbers, or even find metrics for a company's cultural values.

Albrecht died shortly before I started working at Trader Joe's, and it was not long after that, that we got word from the head office of some course corrections. The first round of changes didn't affect me, but I distinctly remember the moment that I got wind of them. Our regional Vice-president, a guy named Greg, came to visit our store, and had a talk in the back room with our Store Captain, Mike.

Because private offices are anathema in Trader Joe's culture, Crew Members often walk in on conversations—for example, other people's reviews —that would be private in almost any other company. I don't know how other people handle these encounters, but I typically just try to get out of earshot as quickly as possible, and I definitely avoid *looking* as if I'm eavesdropping.

Still, while I rooted around in the back room searching for a bottle of wine to fill a customer request, I couldn't help overhearing them. I'd heard one variation or another of the conversation, in many companies, but it was not the kind of thing I expected from Trader Joe's.

It was obvious from the tone and body language involved that it was completely hierarchical; the regional guy was dictating a new policy that the store would be following. I overheard Greg say something like, "So, the Merchants ['merchants' was a term that had previously been management rank occupied by some of the Hawaiian Shirts] will no longer have any management authority, but we're empowering them to lead by example."

It was real corp-speak gibberish, and only my rule about cults not accepting criticism prevented Mike, my Captain, from saying, "Wow, I'm not sure what that means, but it sure sounds like bullshit." I found what I was looking for and got out of the back room, which was suddenly an uncomfortable place to be.

Over the next few days, all the Hawaiian Shirts had short one-to-ones with the Captain, and most of them emerged glum.

Life in the store continued. Changes to the way the store's managers were treated by the company had little direct impact on Crew Members like me, except that I started to notice a little more internecine friction between the Hawaiian Shirts. It was a long time later that I learned that the whole structure of advancement in the company had been dramatically changed.

In the old Trader Joe's, once you got your Hawaiian shirt and became an official 'full-timer,' you were on a pretty clear management track that progressed through several stages beginning with Novitiate and progressing through grades like Merchant to First Mate and finally, Captain. Whenever a new store was opened, a new Captain's position was created and it was filled from the ranks of First Mates. Being a Captain is a six-figure job; there aren't many companies in which a $12 an hour employee can realistically hope to reach such a position.

Just as they would be on a real ship, as full-timers were promoted up through the ranks, they got better pay and more responsibility. It's easy to imagine a numbers guy thinking that by eliminating middle ranks he'd reduce upward pressure on salaries—and eliminate the (relatively) highly paid First Mate position. It's easy to imagine some consultant advising us to, "Get them all competing amongst themselves, and bring out the best in them."

It brought out the worst. Under the old system, most of the Hawaiian Shirts were on a pretty well-understood career track, and they did not feel they were in direct competition with every other full-timer. Cooperation was the norm. For example, the manager in charge of closing the store pushed the crew as hard as possible to leave the store in the best possible shape for whoever had to open it the next morning. That made sense, because some time in the next few days, their roles would be reversed.

Under the new system, each full-timer is in competition with every other full-timer. A Machiavellian assessment is that the Hawaiian Shirts not only don't have much of an incentive to cooperate and proactively assist each other, they might have an incentive to let each other fail, making themselves look relatively better.

Under the old system, anyone in a Hawaiian shirt had management authority over any Crew Member in a mere T-shirt. That was often frustrating to Crew Members, because orders were frequently countermanded faster than they could be carried out, but at least it was clear.

Under the new system, it's far less obvious who actually has management authority. Trader Joe's prides itself on its laid-back vibe and flat management structure. That's cool. It's not clear that anarchy will be as productive a way to run the stores. There's a reason that real ships have sailors and officers, and ranks.

One change that did affect me was in the way Crew Members were reviewed. I'm told that under the old system, Crew Members got a score of between one and five, on five separate criteria. Crew Members weren't just numerically scored; each criterion got a full written paragraph, too. The size of your raise depended on your overall score.

Under the new system, eleven criteria are scored in three broad categories (Customer Experience, Productivity and Quality of Work Performed, and Works as Part of a Team) which could seem like even finer-grained evaluation. But, performance is evaluated only as either 'Acceptable' or 'Needs Improvement.' I got one paragraph of written evaluation in total. Under the new system, everyone who gets 'Acceptable' ratings across the board gets a raise, but it's the same raise for everyone. At my pay grade, it was sixty cents an hour.

Again, the new system keeps a lid on employee costs by eliminating pressure to give big raises to Crew Members who get really exceptional reviews. The new reviews can, no doubt, be prepared quicker than the old ones, too. Those are things a numbers guy can understand.

But since the new system doesn't acknowledge exceptional performance, it doesn't encourage it, either. Every Crew Member quickly gets a sense of which employees represent the threshold of acceptable performance. If you're not going to be acknowledged or rewarded for it, why would you put in more than just an 'acceptable' effort?

If you're running an investment bank, you don't begrudge your employees' huge salaries, because, you figure, they are the ones doing the deals and bringing in the money. They're a profit center. Most numbers guys in the retail category think of front-line employees as a cost center. Why is that? They are, literally, the ones pulling in all the money from customers.

In fairness to Trader Joe's, the company still pays excellent wages for a retailer. (I made $12.50 an hour for most of my time there; my raise to $13.10 exceeded the rate of inflation, and employees who work even 20 hours a week can get medical benefits.)

Even though the changes that took effect at the beginning of 2012 have had an impact on employee morale, and have resulted in some voluntary departures—both of long-term employees, and some of the most promising new employees, too—it's clear that in the prevailing economy, Trader Joe's will have its pick of retail employees for a long time yet.

Companies do, from time to time, let go of the tiller. Companies with strong cultural brands seem particularly prone to it. Starbucks, as we know it today, was entirely the creation of Howard Schultz. When he left the company in 2000, it lost its way. Schultz returned in 2008 and got the company back on course. The company most frequently cited as an example of culture-as-brand is Apple. Steve Jobs was forced out of his own company in 1985; when he returned as 'interim CEO' in the late '90s, Apple was near bankruptcy. With Jobs back at the helm, it became a global brand powerhouse again. Jobs was a notorious micromanager, and the company was a personality cult until his death. It remains to be seen how the company will fare without him at the helm.

So in the end, the questions are... Is Trader Joe's current CEO Dan Bane (an ex-accountant), a numbers guy at heart who was prevented from imposing his own ethos at Trader Joe's by the owner,

Theo Albrecht, a born merchant? Are the changes imposed at Trader Joe's while I worked there indicative of a fundamental change in course? Does the company really believe its own propaganda—that its success is due primarily to its products? It certainly seems as if, to Bane, the crew is a cost center and not a profit center.

Trader Joe's is a big ship, and it will take a long time for it to get off course. But if the answer to those questions is 'yes,' it will eventually find itself in the same rocky waters as the rest of the grocery business.

●●●

About the author

Mark Gardiner lives in Kansas City where he is a partner in re: an advertising agency which specializes in crafting messages that resonate with consumers over 50. For more information about re: please visit www.revolutionaryoldidea.com

In addition to his work in advertising and marketing, he's also one of the world's most respected motorcycle writers. His memoir, Riding Man, is currently in development as a feature film.

●

Questions? Comments?

Please visit www.TraderJoesSecrets.com and follow the link to Reader Community.

Made in the USA
Charleston, SC
04 March 2014